JOURNALING FOR JOY

Writing Your Way to
Personal Growth and Freedom

Joyce Chapman, M.A.

ISBN: 1-4903-8423-5
ISBN-13: 9781490384238

Acknowledgments

Thank you for empowering me to spread the joy! . . .

There are so many extraordinary people and experiences that have brought me to joy! Journal writing has been such a constant source of joy in my life. Special thanks and love to my parents for naming me Joyce . . . it has always empowered me to be joyous! Love and hugs especially go to my family who motivated and encouraged me all along the way. The journalers who have shared their lives, their tears, their joy and their writing with me are warmly thanked and held dear to my heart. I wish to express special appreciation to Diane Chalfant for compiling all the notes, quotes and information from countless journal classes, interviews, teaching materials and student contributions to develop the form of this book.

The identities of the journalers who so generously contributed their work have been changed. My desire and intention is that future journalers may find the value in the wisdom others have achieved through journaling.

To my new editor and partner in the joy of celebration, Nancy Shaw Strohecker—thank you so much for keeping the integrity of this book so high!

And to all my new journaling friends—welcome to the joy!

Oh, please, pay attention to the Joy!

It's always there.
It's the silver lining around the dark cloud.
It's the mother's soft kiss on the scraped elbow.
It's the vision of next year's harvest
In the freshly plowed-under crop.
It's the freedom to grow
That follows the loss.
It's the strength of character that develops
Out of today's terrible tragedy.

Look for it.
Cherish it.
Celebrate it.
Make it the foundation for your growth.

Oh, yes—pay attention to the Joy!

Contents

Preface

Welcome to the adventure of your life. JOURNALING FOR JOY is your takeoff point for one of the most exciting journeys you can ever embark upon—the journey into yourself. On this journey you will be your own personal tour guide. Along the way you will be invited to laugh, cry, remember and let go, and to travel through your past, to acknowledge your present, and to create your future. You will take a close look at who you are now and what you want in your life, inviting your deep inner knowing to come forth. You will assume your rightful position as the main character in your own life. You will determine your future out of conscious choice.

JOURNALING FOR JOY offers a method of journaling in which you, the journaler, will write from your heart and soul with a single focus: to bring your work to the point where *joy* emerges. No matter how much writing it takes to get there, your explicit purpose and intention is to experience the joy that comes from knowing yourself as an intimate friend, and living the life you have created for yourself out of conscious choice.

JOURNALING FOR JOY reveals a special and magical way of molding each of your life's experiences into an outcome of learning and joy. You will move through whatever causes you emotional pain, stress, fear, and confusion until, far back in the distance, you can view it all from the perspective of wisdom and gratitude—as a rich tapestry woven from all the powerful and mundane experiences that have unfolded in your life.

Throughout this book, writing samples of fellow journalers are presented to inspire and, perhaps, touch you with personal glimpses into a shared reality. These writings can serve as a travel guide to prepare the pathway for your journey.

The numerous journal excerpts also allow you the benefit of sitting in on many journaling groups I have facilitated. I am gratefully indebted to the generous sharing of hundreds of journalers whose contributions have laid the foundation for this book, and lent illumination and beauty to its contents.

My own journaling journey began many years ago with a single decision. It was important to be able to produce effective written communications in my work as a school administrator. I signed up for a journal workshop to hone my writing skills.

I approached this first experience with some fear and trepidation: writing for others had always made me uncomfortable. What would they think? How would they judge me? Would I make a good impression? Would I get my thoughts across skillfully? My own standards for judging myself were probably more severe than any outside critic's could ever be. In person and verbally, I communicate comfortably. But to present myself in writing—that was another matter entirely.

I took the workshop hoping that it might help free me from this fear of writing for others. Little did I then suspect what was about to open up for me!

I had long loved to philosophize and create in many areas of my life, but I had never applied those skills to thinking about myself and re-creating my life. By the end of the first day of the workshop, I was amazed to see that I had never paid very close attention to my life.

I realized that until I started thinking about myself in depth, I could not love myself. I didn't know exactly who was there to love! Nor could I love my life, because I didn't know exactly how I felt about it. I had not been paying close attention to what I was feeling and to letting myself feel my feelings. I had never developed the practice of asking myself, "What do *you* think about this?" In many ways, I realized, I was a virtual stranger to myself.

It became increasingly apparent to me that I had not been totally responsible to myself. I had not taken personal responsibility to live my life entirely from choice and to become the person I wanted to be. If I felt sadness, I didn't realize I could intentionally move through it to a different place. If I had a headache, it never occurred to me to write about it—write down to its very source, and then eliminate future headaches by writing new conditions into my life. If I felt victimized, I was unaware that I could write to notice how I had been letting others make my decisions for me, and then take control by envisioning and writing a new chapter in my life!

Unknowing, as I was writing my way through this first journaling workshop, my life had started to change. In becoming a more confident writer, I was becoming a confident creator of my life. I began to ask myself questions and discover my own answers. If I could create my life through writing, I wanted to stop short of nothing less than celebrating life—joyfully—all the time!

Although I have always experienced much joy in my life, I now wanted to be *joy-filled*. I wanted to live my joy perpetually. What a wonderful awareness to realize that I could release my emotions, heal my body, integrate my experience as wisdom, and choose joy out of it all. Journaling led me to realize that joy was mine to choose in each and every moment.

Journal writing invited me to pay serious attention to my life—to ask myself every day, as Ira Progoff has suggested in his book, AT A JOURNAL WORKSHOP, "Where am I in my life right now?" And further: "What is my life telling me right now? Who do I want to be? What do I want? Where do I want to go?"

Often I came upon a lack of necessary information or some belief that blocked me from resolution and taking my next step. I soon discovered not only the importance of journaling to draw out my inner knowingness, but also of reading over what I had written and always asking myself, "What am I learning? When did this begin? Is there someone I could have a conversation with, or some issue I could address that would bring me greater understanding and clarity?"

Self-inquiry and self-discovery have given me more information about myself than if I had read a whole library of books and consulted countless experts. I have found that a lot of time and money spent asking others who you are and what to do can be saved by keeping your own journal!

Thus, journaling became my tool for self-understanding and the method I used to discover inner peace and joy. As I was able to bring greater peace and joy into my life, I naturally realized that my purpose was to make this available to others.

This belief was brought home to me one day when my young granddaughter called, concerned about the threat of nuclear destruction. "If we can get everyone in the world to achieve inner peace and think peaceful thoughts," I said to her, "we can have peace on earth."

"Grandma, will you be in charge of that?" she asked innocently.

I laughed. "What makes you think I can do that?"

"Well, Grandma, if you can't, no one can."

I hung up the phone and said to myself, "She's right, in a way. Who can be responsible for peace in the world, if not each one of us as individuals in our own lives?" From that time on, my focus for everything I did shifted. I knew that my job was to work on myself and, as I grew and expanded, to assist others. JOURNALING FOR JOY was born from this change and commitment.

1

Opening the Treasure Within

The human heart has hidden treasures,
In secret kept, in silence sealed.

—Charlotte Bronte

Is there a treasure in your heart? Is there a poem in your mind? Is there a painting in your vision? Is there a book lurking inside your pen? Is there something in your imagination—waiting to be sung, written, painted, invented or created? The seeds of the gifts we have to give are all there waiting to be nurtured.

Inside us is joy. Something inside knows where our joy lies. We may temporarily forget, but *we do know what we love*. It's natural to be happy. It's natural to be healthy. It's natural to be *alive* and creative. If this is happening in your life, your journal is a wonderful place to write about and play with it. If it isn't happening, then something's getting in the way. Something may be crying out to be resolved. Journal keeping provides a way to discover what is keeping you from feeling healthy, creative, and joyful.

So many external forces pressure us today to look for a high, to look for a way out and to change reality, to be someone other than who we are, not even to be present for ourselves. Journal writing takes us back into our own life, our own experience—to observe, listen, hear and encourage the joy to emerge from within—and then to *enjoy the joy*.

The premise of true joy is simple: what we need to be happy we already have. It will emerge from within when invited and given the chance. It's not to be found outside. It's found by following your heart and following your dream! You are the treasure. You are the joy!

So don't lock up your joy in a box and throw away the key. Journal for your joy. Take out the key, open your journal and accept the invitation to return to your natural self. Discover the treasure inside you.

JOURNALING FOR JOY is a transformational tool with the potential of enhancing personal growth and individual therapy. It provides an internal means for self-inquiry, self-discovery, and self-direction that is unmatched by any external information available to us. It is based on the belief that we are all meant to experience peace, joy and happiness as our natural birthright. Somewhere inside, we know that. We know everything we need to know in order to find it. All it takes is to stop, pay attention and listen to our inner voice.

The inner voice is always there, waiting for the invitation to come out and be heard. Journaling can be the mouthpiece for the inner voice. It becomes a highly personal form of inner work, a work that is yours alone to do. It is the work that brings you home to your own truth, a home where the joy presides.

Everyone can journal. A small child may accomplish journaling by drawing a picture and telling a story, talking about the feelings that go with it, and asking a parent or teacher to write down the words. Those who do not write with ease may speak their thoughts into a tape recorder and then have them transcribed onto paper.

Whatever the circumstances, whenever an individual keeps a journal, there is a way to live life from choice rather than reaction. There is a way to take the driver's seat in life rather than remaining a passive backseat passenger who does not know the destination and is not paying attention to the route. There is a way to be in charge of life and to be joyful.

As human beings we are precious resources containing everything we need to make our lives exactly the way we want them. JOURNALING FOR JOY is a program designed to bring forth your natural beauty, energy, and wisdom, and enable you to live life to your fullest potential.

Be excited about getting to know who you are! Journaling is about your self-expression. It invites you to discover your truth and identify your natural skills, takents, abilities and insights. It welcomes you to discover the answer to the basic question: *Why are you here?* Through the act of writing things down, you allow yourself to wake up, be aware, and pay attention to what your life has to teach you.

Here is what some journalers have had to say about their experiences with journaling:

I Wrote What I Wanted—I Have It Now

Journaling is so special to me. As I reread my journal, I realized again how very much I have grown through this marvelous therapy.

I have received so much JOY from this wonderful release. I have grown in awareness by writing and releasing my thoughts, fears, happiness and sorrow.

Almost everything I have ever wanted, I now have. Through writing in my journal, my affirmations have come true. What I wrote that I wanted in a relationship is what I have in my relationship now. I have found journaling to be the most exciting and quickest way to grow, and I will always write—because it FEELS GOOD!!!

What Seemed Impossible Before

I can't believe the differences in me. I'm in such a state of willingness and openness—ready to expand. What seemed impossible before is probable now.

Opening the Gifts of My Life

Journaling has given me back my *life*. I have wanted to write for a long time, but early reviews frightened me off. I hadn't written since. When I discovered journaling, it just started pouring out. Now, in my sixty-third year, I am finally coming to terms with an extremely harsh and abusive childhood. I am opening the gifts of my life. The more I write, the more I understand.

The Most Important Person

It is only 7:00 A.M. and I've been up since 5:30 writing. I love my journaling. So many truths come out in it. I have learned so much about ME, who I am, how to be more real and true to myself. Maybe most important of all, my journal reminds me every day that *I* am the most important person in my life—if I don't love and respect myself, no one else will either.

Ask, and the Answer Comes

I *use* my journaling. I find that I don't journal every day, but have sessions of one to three hours when I just write on and on. Whenever I need a solution, I ask, journal, and the answer comes. I also draw pictures from time to time, combining that with my journaling. I set my pen to the page, and the truth comes out. My true self talks to me when I journal.

Step Back and Think Things Through

I am a very emotional person. The emotional response is always my first reaction. Through writing I am able to step back from the situation and think things through.

In my consulting work, I frequently encounter people who have lost track of who they are. Often at the price of great pain, they have left behind their dreams, their joy, their aliveness.

This journaling excerpt is from someone who recognized such a separation from self and began her journey back home.

Lost from Myself

Lost from myself
The child in me weeps
And tears flow from adult eyes.
But I will find the light and laughter again.
The secret awaits the search.

The toddler who daily sang on waking
Now sings once a year *Messiah*.
We will recreate each day as Alleluia
When we find again our lost selves.

What journaling is about is taking the time to reconnect with the source of our inner knowing. To return to our true self, we need to spend that hour, day, month, or year on introspection and listening to the inner voice.

The subconscious sometimes offers wonderful gifts of truth from the inner self. You may be surprised and even amazed at what comes out through your pen when you invite your inner self to speak. Rest assured that your inner self holds nothing but the highest truth and good in store for you.

The act of writing makes thoughts become real and brings a deeper level of release than just verbal communication or thinking can do alone. Expressing your thoughts and feelings in writing moves and frees you. Journaling lets go of the heavy internal weights that have held you down. The effect is a lighter and more joyful spirit.

It may not feel at first like journaling is joy. Until you write through all the layers of stored emotional and psychological misperceptions and unload your negative thoughts and beliefs, you may feel like you are drowning, and that devoting any more attention to them will probably pull you under. My advice to you at this critical point is, DON'T STOP WRITING: *journal through it.*

It's important to heal your past. The past is always with you until you do. It keeps coming back in the most unexpected ways. And journaling is a marvelous tool for healing past hurt and pain. But it's even more important to heal *past the wounds*—to get to the place where your *journaling is for joy!* That's the bottom line. That's the ultimate intention. That's what this book is all about.

HOW DO I GO ABOUT JOURNALING, ANYWAY?

Journaling is a natural process. I find there is no right or wrong way to journal. There are no rigid rules, no authority you need to impress and no failing grades. Just let yourself write as you feel and think. Be exactly as you are. Accept and honor whatever comes without judging, censoring or correcting it. Allow your gut reaction or intuition to come forth. Also allow yourself to play, experiment, be humorous, and have fun!

You can write most freely in your journal if you are clear that you are writing for yourself. Remember you are not writing for your spouse or friend, to please a parent or the grade school teacher who suspected all along that you were a writer, or even as a legacy for your children someday. Of course, your writing can be shared with an appropriate and trusted person. But journal writing's main focus is about you and for *you*.

Set no performance standards on yourself as you write. Tristine Rainer in THE NEW DIARY speaks of the "Internal Critic"— that mental specter that always seems to sit in judgment of whatever we do and think. It all too often condemns our efforts, and judges us not quite good enough to measure up to some ideal standard of excellence or perfection. If you invite the Internal Critic to your journaling party, it may take the floor and run the entire show. The young, shy, sensitive, expressive guests from your creative subconscious will be intimidated and will retreat into the shadows.

Ask the critic to wait outside until it is needed. You can call it in when you finish writing what needs to come out spontaneously, and it's time to take the next step of reviewing and evaluating what has come out in your free-flowing writing. That's the function it serves best.

By now, you have probably given some thought to JOURNALING FOR JOY. You'd like to give it a try, and you want to know how to get started. So let's consider the preliminaries.

"But," you say, "I am a terrible speller. I never could write, I have this 'thing' about writing. I never know when to start a new paragraph, and where the commas and apostrophes should go. I've always felt a little embarrassed about my writing."

Thoughts like these often inhibit the beginning journal writer. It is natural to encounter some resistance to journaling, until you begin to discover the immeasurable value it holds for you. Yet one of the purposes of journaling is to remove yourself from judgment and beliefs, and to free up your thoughts and feelings. So cancel out the thought that you can't write well, or that someone else writes better than you.

Dribbling Is a Process of Freeing the Soul

Claire calling her work "dribble" is not OK with me! Every time she has shared, it has given me more permission to *be*. It was believing my work was dribble that kept me stuck for so long. Let's see—is her dribble more *dribbly* than mine?

I have spent most of my life comparing my dribble with other dribbles, and what I now know is that dribbling is a process of freeing the soul. You have to dribble before you can set up to shoot the basket.

Give yourself permission to express your truth, and develop your very own style in doing it.

Permission

An unfolding rosebud
Does not ask permission
For its process.
Wild or domesticated,
Tea rose or miniature,
Each opens to the light
In whatever time it needs
Doing what is required
To release the beauty
That is its essence.

COMMON QUESTIONS ABOUT JOURNAL WRITING

The following is a list of other questions and concerns that are frequently raised about journal writing.

- *What—one more thing I have to impose on myself?*

  Once you begin to reap the rewards of your writing, journaling stops being a burden and often becomes the activity you look forward to most and obtain the greatest value from.

- *I'm afraid someone might read my journal. What should I do about this fear?*

  Hide your journal, or if you've written something you don't want to keep, throw it away or burn it. Remember, it's *your* journal, and it's perfectly OK to keep it private and do whatever you want to do with it. Just know that what you write is of primary interest to yourself. Write *for yourself* and avoid the expectation that someone else will find as much value in your journal as you do.

- *What if I tell myself the truth in my journal and become frightened by the changes I see need to be made in my life?*

  When a writing process wakes us up to our truth, the best way to develop a deeper understanding is to ask for another writing process to learn more. Respect the self-protective function of fear, but give more power to self-expression and free choice than to the fear. Remember, as remote as it may appear, joy is the other side of fear. Journaling can be a healthy companion to seeking therapy or the aid of a professional during difficult times, too.

- *Someone told me that journaling can make people emotional, and sometimes even makes them cry.*

  Yes, that's true, but being emotional is a healthy, cleansing part of the process. Held back tears may need to flow. Grief withheld may need to be experienced. Pent-up anger may need to be resolved. Emotions and tears may be released as the writing taps into deeper undercurrents of the psyche. If these emotions seem too overwhelming, consider seeking professional help.

- *Would I ever want to read all this stuff?*

  Your writing may simply serve the purpose of clearing out the clutter from your mind—a worthwhile result even if it is never read again. On the other hand, writing that at first seems purposeless may lead to valuable insights as your ideas develop. Rereading your writing later and observing what occupied your mind at a particular time is often very meaningful and instructive.

- *I used to keep a diary, but I never saw much point in writing down everything that happened every day. And I felt so guilty about times I didn't write that it was a relief when I finally stopped.*

JOURNALING FOR JOY is a natural process that goes beyond this kind of routine recording or logging of the day's events. It leads you to examine and extract the feelings and meaning behind your experiences. The journaler synthesizes the value and the learning without imposing any sense of judgment or obligation. No matter what or when you write, the main criterion is to use your experience to learn more about yourself, and uncover the joy that lives inside you.

GUIDELINES FOR MAXIMIZING THE USE OF YOUR JOURNAL

As you read this book, you may do any or all of the journal exercises as they relate to your personal needs and circumstances. You can pick up the book, turn to any chapter or page, and begin reading and writing. The purpose of this book is to spark your interest and facilitate you on your inner journey, so please make it your own. Feel free to mark the pages liberally, noting ideas inspired by the material you read. Jot down topics for future writing you want to do, journaling questions you want to ask yourself, and results you want to achieve through your own writing. The greatest value you can obtain from reading this book will be the insights you receive afterward from your very own writing.

What kind of book or binder should the journaler use for writing? That depends on your own personal preferences. I recommend using whatever type of notebook, pen, and paper—lined or blank—you feel most comfortable with. A three-ring notebook allows flexibility for inserting and moving pages around.

Dating your journal entries gives you invaluable reference points for looking at both your writing and yourself from a historical perspective. Even if a date doesn't seem important at the time you're writing, it may take on importance later. A date positions each piece of your writings in its proper context and demonstrates the evolution of your thoughts and feelings.

Whenever possible, set aside uninterrupted time for journaling in a space that is free from distractions, so you can really be with yourself. Ask yourself, "In the midst of fully living my life, am I worth the time it takes to pause and consciously choose joy out of every life experience?" Allow yourself to be your own teacher. Learn to turn to your journal and trust yourself.

Write with the underlying premise that you choose truth, aliveness, and joy. *Read over everything* after you write it. End each writing session with a *Feedback Statement* that summarizes your response to your work as you now see it. Your *Feedback Statement* may begin with: "I learned . . ." "I saw . . ." "I now realize . . ." "My next step is . . ." *Feedback Statements* can become a way to love and honor yourself and to acknowledge your learning.

Use your writing for further self-inquiry and discovery. Ask yourself, What is the *feeling* tone in my writing? What does this piece say to me? What action or further writing needs to take place? For example, one journaler wrote as feedback to herself, "This depressing, 'stuck' piece does not express who I am or where I want to be. I want a spirit as free as a bird. I want to fly like an eagle. My soul longs to take flight. I will watch birds fly today and record my observations. I want to write a conversation with an eagle in my journal."

SOME BENEFITS OF JOURNAL WRITING

In addition to all that's been said so far, so many more practical benefits are derived from journaling that it's a challenge to conceive of them all at once.

Why journal? To find the missing pieces; say the unsaid; understand your process; reach into the hidden recesses of your self; achieve clarity, direction, and certainty in your life; to move forward out of chaos and confusion into focus and balance. One of the greatest reasons is that journaling reveals the patterns of thoughts, feelings, and behaviors in your life. I remember many years ago asking my children in a kindergarten class, "Why are you learning the alphabet?" One child answered clearly, "So someday I can learn to read and have more choices." Why learn to journal? So you can understand your own patterns, and this understanding will make more choices available to you. Why journal? For JOY!

Here are some of the many important results you can achieve through journaling:

- To know who you are.

- To turn problems into opportunities, gifts.

- To learn to trust yourself as your own counselor.

- To release feelings, turmoil, stress.

- To access information from your subconscious mind.

- To find answers to what seems to be unanswerable.

- To capture the teachings of your past.

- To record experiences and thoughts you want to keep and remember.

- To awaken the writer's voice within you.

- To communicate with others when talking is difficult or impossible.

- To integrate what you are learning from a class, lecture, or life situation.

- To know yourself as a spiritual being.

- To heal the past.

- To live from being awake and aware of the present.

- To create the future by conscious choice.

- To understand the connection between thought and health.

- To understand your "partners" in life.

- TO CAPTURE THE JOY!

YOUR FIRST JOURNALING EXERCISE

So, you are ready to set off on your own personal JOURNALING FOR JOY adventure. Why not begin by answering the following questions for yourself: How do I feel right now about journal writing, and what I would like journaling to do for me? Date your writing and give it a title. Write as little or as much as you want, in any way you like. When you finish, read your work over and write yourself a *Feedback Statement* that sums up what you learned and what your next step is.

Congratulations! You are on your way.

2

A Daily Record to Capture
the Meaning of Your Life

"Mr. and Mrs. Jones are now happily married, as the ship's gong chimes midnight and only a few late longing lovers linger about under the stars on deck. Steady on course for the north northeast, light wind out of the southwest at 5 knots; all is quiet and calm."

The captain of a ship records in the ship's log every significant detail of position, weather, and notable happenings among passengers and crew. The record of the journey will be the tool used to correct the ship's course in the future and to plan improvements in subsequent voyages.

As captain of your life cruise, you too can keep a log of your experiences and the sights you see. When you read it over, weeks, months or even years later, your writing may provide a treasured record of fond memories that takes you right back to the foghorn and the salty taste of the ocean spray, the mysterious fascination of someone you met at a banquet, the day you wandered exhilarated through a distant port city.

Even though you may not be sailing on a luxury ocean liner today, the choice to make each moment just that valuable is no less your choice or decision. Appreciation of our learning and our joy is inherent in each day's experience. It is brought out by the power of *directed intention* when we keep a written record of our events, feelings, thoughts, and what it all means.

A good starting point for beginning to keep a daily record is to sit down at the end of your day and picture the day's events in the context of the "ocean cruise" of your life. Review your day. Close your eyes, letting the day pass before your attention on the movie screen of your mind. Go back to the time when you were still in bed. Recall your first thought of the morning. Notice how your body felt. What was your first movement of the day? What was the first thing you did? What did you look forward to or dread? What would an objective outside observer think, watching your movements? What might not appear obvious to an observer, being known only to you? What interactions did you have with other people? Where did you go? What were your thoughts? What happened next? What were the feelings you felt? What did you notice about your body?

When you feel ready, open your eyes and write your thoughts about your day. Describe who you were. What was it like to be living your life? What was your life about? Go back over your daily appointment book or calendar and recreate your day, adding feelings, colors, sounds, sights—the stage, scenery, drama, characters, interactions.

Did you keep a diary as a teenager, only to read it later and consider it a silly, useless exercise in trivialities? The daily journal you begin today will be different in a very important way: you will add your interpretation of the significance of the events you record. You will use your writing to glean insights and bring richness into your life.

When you have recorded the main ideas and details of your day's experiences, stop and reread what you have written. What does it say to you? What conclusions can you draw? What action is suggested?

Microcosm of My Life

I awoke several times in the night, aware that my body was feeling the effects of fighting off a mild cold. I started to say a prayer of alignment, but no sooner had I claimed to accept God's perfect peace and radiant health, than several troubling matters popped into my head, forcing me to realize that, indeed, I was out of alignment with that ideal spiritual harmony. I had allowed fear and worry to set in—fear of finances, vicarious fears from the San Francisco earthquake disaster, and anger at the poor handling of arrangements by the airline I just traveled on.

I gathered my fears under an umbrella and reassured myself that, with God's help, I could handle whatever comes up. I fell back asleep and dreamed that my father was grasping my shoulders, holding me at arm's length, looking into my eyes and saying, "You were my great hope. Then you left and never came back. I missed you so much." A peculiar dream, because I don't think my father would ever have felt or said this. (Would I want him to?) What does it mean?

The morning was normal and routine. I felt glad, as I always do, to be living pleasantly and peacefully now, most of the time. At work, Rozalyn was exceptionally cheerful. She figured out how to do the inventory calculations on her own, and has proceeded with several pages independently of my assistance. I was energized by her enthusiasm and pride.

Parking at the post office, a driver squealed into the parking place I was just about to take, slamming his brakes an inch from my front bumper. I had that sinking feeling: will he hit me, and could I prevent it? I knew I would never have reacted quickly enough. (Does everyone slip into that sort of altered reality when they watch, almost as a passive observer, almost with gruesome fascination, to see if the inevitable will happen?) I recovered in time to roll my window down and call out somewhat sarcastically, "Thank you." He seemed embarrassed by his excessively aggressive move. Overall, I was still riding on the morning's cushion of positive energy, so the incident remained but a brief, passing encounter, and didn't upset my well-being.

Not to dream about it anymore, I wrote a complaint/suggestion letter to the airline, asking reimbursement for extra expenses incurred. I notice I write wonderful complaint letters after somebody jars me. Now I can drop *that* problem, anyway. What else do I need to clear up, to bring my mind back into alignment and throw off these cold symptoms? This weekend I'll work on the financial records I must prepare by Monday. And why do I listen and endlessly fill my mind with the trauma of the earthquake victims? Does vicarious suffering help anyone? I'll send a donation check instead.

In the evening, we watched the movie *Clara's Heart*. It seemed to be missing pieces, such as any interaction between the mother and son, and the inexplicable abrupt skip to a happy ending. Still,

I like movies that touch the heart, and it was good to feel such an intimate glimpse into a child's pain and cares. The Jamaican culture presented a fascinating picture, too. I'm glad for movies that make us *feel* for each other.

Frank seemed indifferent, as he often does to the shows I like to watch. We seem rather estranged lately; just writing this makes me realize we need to have a good, close talk.

Feedback: My body is a perfect reflection of the assortment of slight upsets that have been filling my mind. Many of these matters can be dealt with and set aside. My day had its ups and downs —a microcosm of my life. Not 10's and 1's, but more like 4's and 6's. I lived much of the day *responding* to others rather than choosing my reality and then creating it.

I once came home from one of the many never-ending, pointless meetings I was required to attend and immediately sat down to record the day's events. After writing, I realized that I hated everything about the meetings I attended and that I no longer fit in that organization. There was no further contribution I could make, and I definitely didn't need to be sitting in meetings making judgments and hating it, if nothing could be done to change things. The next day, I resigned.

Breakthroughs come when we record our experience in enough depth to become aware of where we are and what changes we need to make. When we record our lives, we start to take responsibility for what happens in our lives. I don't know how many more meetings I would have sat through without realizing that the time for action was long overdue—if it weren't for that simple act of recording. Up to that point, I had remained stuck in my feeling responses, and the judgment and criticism I felt for the whole situation. My writing brought me back to my*self* and my truth.

By keeping a daily record, you will soon notice that you remain in constant dialogue with your life. Your journal becomes the daily newscast of your life, filling you in on the latest information, resources, and recommendations. And you can talk back to your life, drawing from its teachings, testing out its feedback and giving it direction. You have an opportunity to constantly question, "If this is my life, do I like it? Do I want to change it?"

Time Ticking Away

I awake aware of the cool air drifting in through the open window. The sheet is cool and crisp. I get up, knowing I have overslept. My mind is full of ideas about how to improve my life. I want to exercise but I don't make the time. I sleep late and rush to work. I don't wear my watch and ask everyone what time it is all day. I go out to dinner and am late to class. Even at lunch with Sherry, I have to ask her to tell me when it is five minutes to one.

Time is on my mind. The clock ticks and rings on the hour. Every minute does count. The message I see today is that my life is ticking away just like the clock. As I move through each day, every minute is important. I am not reaching my potential and I am impatient. I don't want to wait any longer.

I am at work typing on the computer, and the words come into my mind, "FATAL ERROR." Phil and Dale are talking about "fatal errors." I want to research computer language. I want to change the words these machines are programmed to use. I've never seen "LOVE" come up on the screen. The word *love* is not "acceptable" in business—Wow! An article on this might make lots of programmers laugh.

Time management is the issue I'm dealing with today. I drift through my life so much. I make plans for a weekend and then don't get anything done. Do I ever do the things I really want to do?

As you experiment to find the method of daily recording that works best for you, another technique to try is to carry a small notebook with you throughout the day, and make notations as you go along. This on-the-spot record will give your daily journal a fresh sense of immediacy, and will provide an invaluable data base for reviewing the ongoing circumstances and direction of your life.

Be sure to scan through your daily records at the end of the week —and month—and take advantage of the cumulative messages that are there for you. As a keeper of a daily record in your journal, you will learn immensely from your writing over time.

FRAMING A MEMORY

Some days may be truly special in a way that you'll want to capture and preserve their uniqueness in your journal. The following writer planned a party for the explicit purpose of replacing her sadness with joy. When the party was over, she began to feel the old, familiar letdown. She knew from past experience where her thoughts were likely to lead next. Instead of becoming depressed, she decided to make a word portrait of her joy and frame it to remember.

The Party's Over

Midnight—the party is over, but the memories linger. Friends, great friends. Family, great family. A time for sharing, a time for giving—giving of our love for one another on this holiday occasion. Laughter, gaiety, festivity. A hope that through this sharing of lighter moments may come better understanding, closeness, bonds that cement our relationships securely for the future.

It was a compatible group—a cross-section of many walks of life, converging harmoniously into one whole. For a brief moment we were one in purpose, sharing not only the fruit of God's abundance, but his goodness in bringing us together to relate on a human level.

The evening was a success. Good food, good drink, good company. The coming together of good friends to celebrate the holiday season occasioned by the birth of the Lord. For through Him all things come together in His name.

YOUR DAILY RECORD IS A TAKEOFF POINT

Your daily recording will generate the ideas for much of the rest of your journaling work. Say you're standing in line at the grocery store and you overhear two people talking with an Australian accent. You think, "Australia must be a fascinating place to see." You drive away, and the thought vanishes. But if you're a recorder, you will come home and write, "One of the most interesting things today was my reaction to seeing these people from Australia. I want to go to Australia!" Soon, you may go to a travel agency and get information about Australia. Your writing may move you to follow through on a vague yearning, to make it a concrete possibility.

Like the song that keeps singing over and over in your mind, until you finally stop and pay attention, the event or interaction that occupies your mind can come out as valuable information when you write about it. What is it in that song that wants to be remembered or resolved?

I was talking with a journaler on the phone one day who told me, "I feel like a wounded bird." She decided to write about times in her life when she felt like a wounded, helpless bird.

Wounded Bird

I am a little wounded bird. I've fallen from my nest. I have scratches all over. I am bleeding, and my wings are clipped. I can't fly. I am hurt and scared, and so vulnerable.

I want to be protected. I want to be picked up and held by someone with big, strong hands. I want to be loved and taken care of. I don't want to be hurt anymore. I don't want to fall or be pushed out/around anymore.

I want my scratches to heal and my wing fixed. I want to become a beautiful grown-up bird, and fly to the highest altitudes.

I will build a new nest, a nicer and bigger nest that is safe, with guard-rails. After I'm settled there, I want to invite new birds into my life. These new birds will be kind, honest, motivated, inspired, happy, and prosperous. We'll fly together.

Feedback: I'll never need to write a wounded bird piece, ever again—or return to that awful old story!

After writing this piece, this person realized, "I have been a wounded bird my entire life!—but no more!" It was a life-impacting revelation that came out of a simple phone conversation which could easily have passed by unnoticed.

The following writer had become quite practiced in observing and paying attention to her inner signals. She noticed that a small, overly insignificant interaction with a friend had stuck with her all day. Knowing this was a sure sign that there must be something of value to be learned from it, she decided to take it to her journal.

Finding the Significance in an "Insignificant" Event

I "pushed" Carla today. I felt invited to push her. She trusts me and wants support. What did I learn? That I am a better pusher than "pushee." I am better at focusing on other people's lives. It takes the pressure off me. Carla was easy to push because she is so open.

Feedback: Learn to be more open, and allow others to support me too.

Any unrest that comes up in the moment can be dealt with and learned from by writing in your daily record. It may be a simple reaction to a picture you see in a magazine or a deep response to something in the news. It may be an observation you make in the grocery store or while driving on the freeway.

Fly With Me

The eagle soars high above the majestic mountains.
Wings spread—warm air caressing his feathers.
His green eyes—so sharp, so clear.
But he cries for the death
Of what he loves so dear.

His life is in danger—
No friend, apart from the gift of life.
What has happened, oh eagle?
What has happened to cause such strife?

You are a prisoner—trapped in man's tight grasp.
I wish I could unlock the chains and set you free . . .
But look, oh eagle, they've trapped even me . . .

Together we'll suffer, share a mutual sea of tears.
We'll cry and die inside, though no one ever hears.

Eagle, I see you flying high above,
Carried by the breeze.
Eagle, dear eagle, fly with me.
Across the open seas.

(This passage is because I love nature and cry over its destruction.)

If you find yourself impassioned by a particular social or political issue, or an event you encounter in your everyday life, use your journal to let these feelings pour out. Then later, follow up this work further: What issue of yours does this speak to? Take a poignant line from your piece and write another piece exploring it. The writer of the poem might write of herself "being trapped in a tight grasp," or of what it would be like to be "flying high above." She might respond to the anger she feels about the destruction of nature, or about the "eagle" in her that is being extinguished. After speaking of her reaction to the piece she has written, she might want to conclude by asking herself, what action might this writing suggest?

KEEPING A LOG FOR EVERY OCCASION

"How can I know myself?" people often ask when they begin on their self-discovery process. They may be acute observers of others, but they do not direct their attention onto observing themselves. When I taught young children, I would tell them jokingly, "Your ticket to come in tomorrow will be to know what color your mom's eyes are. All who know their telephone numbers will get their names added to the *I Know* list." I would encourage them to become aware of the world around them. And, of course, they would laugh and come to school knowing more than they knew the day before—also more lively and more *involved* in their life.

One of the simplest ways to observe yourself is by keeping a log, or simple list recording the details you're interested in knowing more about. When you choose to be more aware, follow through with a concrete action: set the facts and figures down in black and white before you. What are you dissatisfied with? What do you feel unfulfilled about? What area would you like to assume more control over? What feeling or experience do you want to increase in your life? Make a log, and begin recording the raw data you will have to work with.

Author George F. Simons in his book KEEPING YOUR PER-SONAL JOURNAL recommends asking, "If I could take a souvenir or memento from today, what would it be?" and "Is there something I would like to say to each person who entered my day in some form?" Wonderful learning can come from recording the activities and thoughts and events of one single day:

1. Want to become more positive? Log your negative thoughts and words for a day. Then write what your learning is from what you have observed.

2. Log your accomplishments for a week, and then write a *Feedback Statement*.

3. Keep a log of your frustrations during a day at the office or at home. Then write what you can learn from what you have written.

4. Want to learn to communicate more effectively? Keep a log of your communications for a day, and then write yourself a *Feedback Statement*.

5. What's bugging you? Keep a log for a day, and then write your conclusions and recommendations to yourself.

6. Your body is acting up again? Keep a record of your symptoms for a day or a week, noting alongside each what else was going on in your life at that time. At the end, write what learning is available from this record. Then keep another log: of times your body feels wonderful!

7. Keep a record of your loving encounters for a day or two: what message comes through your writing?

8. Want to learn to be more assertive? Keep a log of your interactions for a day. Ask yourself, "Did I say what I felt, wanted, needed? Or did I say, 'What's the use?' or 'Who cares.' 'What difference does it make?' "

9. Low self-esteem? Keep a log for a day of thoughts and interactions that raised and lowered your self-esteem. What is the
   learning there?

10. Is self awareness an issue for you? Keep a log for a day of your
    state of energy, moment to moment. Write a *Feedback State-
    ment* about what your observations say to you.

11. Keep a log of your feelings for a day. What do you conclude?
    Write about your learning. If there is a feeling you want to
    increase in your life, keep a log of the times you experience
    this feeling. Is your life too bland? Keep a log of times you
    experience passion. Summarize your conclusions.

   In a brainstorming session, I once encouraged participants to list
every kind of log they had ever used or would like to use. The list cov-
ered an entire wall. You could think of an infinite number of ideas for
logging. If you keep a log of what you did in your garden this year and
how it turned out, you could improve your garden next year. If you
have a weight problem and cannot remember what you have eaten
today, you might want to start a food log. If you want to increase your
exercise, how about an exercise log?—give yourself gold stars! If you
want to recapture the romance in your relationship, begin a romance
log.
   If you want to find out what's going on in your life that causes you
so much conflict, keep a conflict log. Were you criticized? Did someone take something you wanted? Were you unable to do what you
wanted? Were you unappreciated? List these incidents, what the issue
was, who was involved, and what you wanted. When conflicts persist,
they can turn into complaining, gossip, and symptoms of physical ill-
ness. Your conflict log will lead you to root out the causes of conflict.
When you keep this log, action will follow to resolve the problem.
   Do you have habits you would like to change? Catch yourself sub-
stituting new behaviors, and keep a log of what you did. Keep a
phone log, to find out how much time you spend on the phone, and
with whom. Keep a log of addictive behaviors, and the thoughts and
feelings that preceded them each time. Note and write down any
judgmental and critical remarks, and the effects they produced. Log

your mistakes and what you learned from them. And how about a log of "Erase Its"—what you would like to be able to erase from the day (that second brownie, those harsh words with a loved one, the job left undone). Then try logging your wins, your successes, your accomplishments.

As you look over a log, you will begin to notice patterns and see relationships between thoughts, feelings and actions. By becoming the observer, you then become the planner, the designer, the critiquer and the organizer. Logging captures the details that point to a powerful realization: Aha! I'm in charge of my life! I create my own mental environment. Logging is a great self-empowerment tool.

Daily Log—What Is Life Teaching Me?

- Got a phone call from Marsha.

- Lynn called to tell me Mary Kay cosmetics are 30% off.

- Phone company called to respond regarding address.

- Owner of the designer clothes company said I could not have the color pattern I wanted.

- Picked up mail—boring! Still no flyer from church.

- Watched my video and loved it!

- Took Cathy to voice class.

- Saw movie with Bob.

- Received package from editors and took note to Deb regarding her book.

- Returned Robin's phone call.

- Took clothes to cleaners'; laughed with the counter lady!

- Saw graffiti that said "Invest in Body Bags."

- Watched PBS—inspired by excellence of researcher's work.

    What a wonderful life I have!

Too often we allow our lives to pass by without integrating the details we encounter. The moment passes, and the information is lost. Logging gives us a means of recording the important details of our experience, and using them to learn and progress in our lives. Logging gives a focus and an emphasis to our experience.

When you start logging, you will find many categories of information that are valuable to record. I keep a secion in my journal for recording great ideas I read in books and see in movies. You may like to set aside separate pages in your journal for any of these idea logs:

- a short synopsis of books read and their important ideas

- quotes to remember

- memorable thoughts from a class or lecture

- amusing anecdotes, jokes and cartoons

- ideas on latest projects

- inventions and creations

- dreams

- ideas for making money

- ideas to use in presentations or papers you will write

- ideas for books you may want to write

Other useful logs are ideas of "Aha!" insights that strike you suddenly when you are driving or doing something else, and a log of "shower" ideas—ideas that flash in when you're in the shower. Take just a moment to jot these ideas down, and plan to go back over them later.

My Morning Shower Log

- Would love to go to France in May. Thought of the perfect travel outfit—and Katie would be there. Hopefully, she'd be speaking French by then!

- So glad the vase the cat broke was not valuable.

- Thought about how much I love Dad being here. He wants to make furniture—what a great idea!

- My birthday is in two days. I want to go see Cirque du Soleil with a man.

    Feedback: Isn't it great that I'm not worried about making my house payment. I'm so glad I have clean thoughts in the shower!

I have suggested that clients keep a thinking log, a log of all their thoughts over a period of time without any interference from radio or TV. A time period of fifteen minutes each hour will make you aware of your "mind chatter" and the patterns in your thinking. One person reported afterward, "I hate it. These thoughts stink. I have got to change my thinking and my life!"

USE YOUR LIFE AS A LEARNING LABORATORY

People have told me, "I have shelves and shelves of my diaries, just sitting there gathering dust." All too often, they reveal that they have written with no purpose in mind. It has become a useless, somewhat compulsive ritual.

"I've kept a journal all my life, but it's never *taught* me anything," they say. When I suggest using their writing as a learning experience, they're surprised and curious. It's a small but very critical step to reread a journaling piece and draw out the learning from it.

In journaling, when you become aware of the decisions you have made and are about to make, there is a fascinating side-effect: you begin to *act* out of this new awareness. "What will I write about this in my journal?" becomes a question that impacts the decision itself.

For example, you are wrapped in a heavy embrace, half-heartedly considering, "How far should I let this go?" A cartoon bubble flashes before your eyes: the image of a blank page in your journal. You start to think of the present moment in terms of the journaler, the observer, the recorder. This may be a life decision that you will either cherish or regret if it is made unconsciously. What would you learn from it if you were writing about it right now? What feelings and thoughts would weigh in your decision if you journaled beforehand?

Logically extended, then, you not only make a wiser decision at that moment, but you begin also to write in advance about situations you anticipate coming up soon. Do I skip work today? Do I let this little white lie slip by? Do I really need to finish this homework tonight, when it's so late and I'm so tired? Should I turn the alarm off and go back to sleep? Should I stay in school—*will* I stay in school, the way I'm going right now? Can I dull the pain?—should I get drunk or use drugs just this once? Small decisions—but first steps down a new road, each one. You become the director and the designer of your life when you write about decisions you will be making that might change the course of your life.

Recently, a series of cancellations and changes were phoned in to me: a class I had counted on teaching fell through because of too few enrollments; a group consultation had to be postponed; two private clients canceled appointments; a printing that needed to get in the mail couldn't be completed. At an earlier time in my life, I would probably have looked at all this with a sense of anxiety and failure. Since I have trained myself through my journaling to say, "How is this perfect? What am I learning? What does this free me up to do?", I responded far differently. My job is to take this learning and go forward with it—so that I don't just repeat old patterns unconsciously. When you use your life as a learning laboratory, you move beyond experiencing yourself as a passive victim of its circumstances; you make the best of whatever is available and grow from it.

In the school classrooms where I used to teach, a specific time period was set aside every day when we all wrote in our journals and then shared from our work. The time following this period was always tranquil and unified because we had each expressed our inner concerns, and we all knew where we stood and what we were dealing with. I can only imagine the changes that might be made in this world if we all began making a regular practice of daily recording.

3

Snapshots of Your Life—
An Album of Memories

"So much of my life has been so rich, but I never wrote any of it down," a middle-aged woman said to me, with tears beginning to form in her eyes.

"Don't worry," someone else advised her. "It's all there, in your memory somewhere. The experiences are not lost; they may be just 'deep on the disk.' As you write, the memories will begin to return." In the words of an eighty-three-year-old woman who began to journal about her childhood, "The more I write, the more I remember. The more I remember, the more I remember."

Precious Moments

"Precious moments, do not fade away into forgotten obscurity." Last night I awoke at 2:00 a.m. with this sentence on my mind. "I'll journal on that," I wrote, and went back to sleep with a happy plan to write about the delights and enthusiasms of my ten-year-old child.

In the same way you stop and take a snapshot of something in life you want to remember, *what if*, from the earliest age you had also recorded the significant moments and experiences in writing? What if, every time you looked at this record you were able to remember the learning of that moment? What if, as a young child, you were taught to be responsible for the learning you brought with you from the day before? What if you kept a running record of what worked and what didn't work? Your life would be your lesson plan. Your learning would be integrated into your life each day. By being a faithful observer, you will learn to chronicle your life and, over time, perhaps you will learn to choose the joy.

Many notable private journals have provided important historical records, as well as personal glimpses into the life and times of a different age. A good example is the incredible writing left by the diary of Anne Frank, a legacy of the indomitable human spirit holding fast to life and love through the darkest hours of human history. Benjamin Franklin once said, "The next thing most like living one's life over again seems to be a recollection of that life, and to make that recollection as durable as possible by putting it down in writing."

The recollection is valuable not just for its own sake, but as a resource to draw from for learning and joy.

The Echo of a Time I Lost

On a trip to the Caribbean two years ago, I had a strange experience. I was standing on the bridge of a ship moving slowly through the Panama Canal. Friends by my side were talking about the intricate and marvelous engineering of the locks. The lush shore, palm trees, houses on stilts, seemed every bit as familiar to me as the back of my hand. I had an intense feeling of coming home. My flesh tingled; my breath sang a lullaby. This feeling overcame me so, that I could not share it. I just hugged it to me and held it close to my heart.

Whether you want to keep a record of significant events of the past, or are writing to document or describe a present experience, your journal is a wonderful place for preserving the moment, and for summarizing what you have gained from it. We are the accumulation of what has gone on before us, and our past unfolds endless new revelations to teach us about our present. We have but to open up this 'album of memories,' and begin forming the pictures into words.

YOUR STORY

Recording a memory is an excellent way of opening up the window into journaling about your personal history. Often in classes people will tell me, "My whole past is just a blur," or, "I can't remember a thing that happened before I was eighteen—how can I write about early memories?" But as they start to write, they discover that their memories are the very window to their soul. The writer's voice that was blocked and silent is now set free.

When I first began to journal, I made about an hour of undisturbed time for myself and wrote on the question, "What's buried in my memory that would be enjoyable to recall and could tell me something about my past?" I closed my eyes for a moment, and a thought came to write about my high school graduation. "It was fun," I thought at first, "but I don't remember very much from that long ago." As I started to write, more and more of the details came to me. By the time I finished, I found that I had re-created a precious and joyful memory that I would love rereading in my journal from time to time.

Graduation Day

It was late afternoon. The excitement in the air was lifting us all right off the ground. I felt tall and beautiful in my gleaming white high heels. Everyone was so full of life and so trusting, ready for whatever life had in store for our future. (Just like today!)

I was seventeen and on top of the world. I had never stopped to question my life, just rushed into each new day and lived it fully as it came to meet me. Mom always made sure I was properly dressed, so I would present myself to the world as beautifully as possible.

Lyndon was the boy I was in love with, and our relationship was in constant turmoil. Did we ever really communicate? I doubt it—that would be fun to look at in another writing.

Back on the lawn: we were all sparkling and laughing. John was organizing the group in his wonderful way. Who else was there? The whole gang: Sammy, Jackie, Sally, Kay, Wilbur, Frank, Bill, Janet, Joanie, Jerry, Marlene, Jo, Katie, Crillene, Bill, Barbara, Nancy, Peter, Ann, and Lou.

So much had been going on over the previous weeks, all the preparations for this grand event. Twelve hundred were graduating—lots of world changers, that's for sure.

The folding chairs and new high heels sank into the grassy lawn. We all had new clothes under our royal blue gowns, our white tassels dangling, carefully balanced on the proper side of each blue cap. My dress, a matter of great importance then, was white organdy with gray eyelets, lined with a soft gray slip.

What an important event this was for my dad! He had a suit on, *so proud* that his pride and joy, *me*, was graduating from high school and going on to college. I was his hope for the future.

I got my pearls as a gift. Thanks, Mom. They were so beautiful—still are, as a matter of fact.

I remember so well the joy, the fun, the excitement, and all the aliveness I felt at that time in my life. It was a very happy and vital time for me—and I know this is still who I am today.

You have your collection of old pictures and old memories of faces. How powerful it can be for you to put these memories into words, and then capture the essence of the experience in a *Feedback Statement*.

Continuing to look through your photo album of memories from the past, you may see a picture of your best childhood friend. The memories begin to flood back as you think of shared experiences with this person.

A Special Person to Remember

I drove by Suzanne's old house today, on purpose because I had thought of her earlier. Oh, what a special friend Suzanne was in my life. What laughter and great learning we shared, overcoming incredible challenges together. She created the 'pity parties' so we could all get together and laugh at our predicament. She was my very best friend.

And what a giver she was—making sandwiches for Louise's wedding, loving Carlos because he taught her cats to do the cha-cha. I remember the day she told me she was getting married—how her eyes sparkled and we danced around hugging wildly. And the day she told me the newest outrage about what our supervisor had done, and she got chewed out for using "inappropriate language" when she called him a nerd. We could laugh and laugh at any passing thought—a lot of words were not needed.

Then, too, what a temper she had! I remember her dressing up in a big, bright red envelope to play "Big Red" in Joey's kindergarten class when they were learning their colors. It was funny, because everyone knew why she was red. She was famous for her ability to rant and rave. In fact, she taught *me* to rant and rave— and we made our problems into fun. Few friends have meant so much to me.

Feedback: Memories of Suzanne remind me how important good friends are to me, and how they have shaped my life.

The retelling of your story is similar to the chapters of a history book. You may have had a main character whose role was overshadowed by events. There may be threads that reappear frequently throughout the book. The capturing and marking of an event, as well as defining the ending and beginning, allow you to complete that chapter of your life. With that completion comes freedom—the freedom to choose joy!

The Love Is Gone

My finger has a ridge
Where my wedding ring was
For almost twenty-five years.
My heart also has ridges
Marking memories stored inside
A new ring for each hot or dry year.

My marriage is over.
Sometimes I wonder
How long I was happy
Or if I always lied
And made believe there was love.
Was there? Inside?
Ever?

The love is gone.
It died.
And I have not even cried.

The ridge on my finger
Will fade away
Like the marriage
That ended yesterday.

YOUR LIFE FROM ANOTHER POINT OF VIEW

In video feedback work where the camera records the action, people learn to critique themselves as if they were totally objective observers. They become detached. In journaling also, writing about your own past experience in the third person, as if you were writing about someone else, is a valuable technique to use. When I started doing this, I realized it freed me up. It got me out of my "graded," analytical self. This kind of writing doesn't allow you to sink down in the mire of your pain and your draining drama. You view your events as if they are a story unfolding on TV.

In Crafts Class

Joyce was in her third year of high school, and one of the highlights of that period in her life was crafts class, with its relaxed, easygoing atmosphere. So different from the high-pressured push of all her other college prep classes, crafts class offered a release and a time to be true to her natural ability.

As she passed by the snack shack and walked down the long hall to the crafts room, Joyce's thoughts would inevitably turn to Jerry, and she looked forward to sitting next to him with the pure delight of close friendship. There was nothing sexual about such a friendship. She didn't have to smell good for Jerry. She didn't have to have curly hair and a great-looking outfit on for him. There was nothing to prove with Jerry. There was no competition between them. Highly competitive in the race for top grades and social recognition and everything else, Joyce felt different with Jerry. Such concerns never entered into their friendship. As class partners, they worked side by side, in the uncomplicated exhilaration of pure play.

Feedback: In writing this, I feel reconnected with all I learned in those fun and exciting years. With Jerry I found out how important it was—and still is—for me to be with people who totally accept me. These are the memories that have shaped me into the person I am today. I want to be sure I have lots more fun memories to capture.

After you finish writing a piece in third person, it may then be valuable to rewrite it in first person, noticing the changes in feelings that this shift in writing brings about.

RELEASE THE PAST

When I realize I am hanging on too long to emotional pain from the past, my approach becomes, "Get it out now, and let's deal with it!" Writing about the skeletons in your closet can be an effective way to reduce their hold on you. Once your secret feelings are dragged out of the dark and captured on paper, you have a way to begin to deal with and release them.

Step into the Sunlight

"Shame on you! . . . Shame, shame," the mother of the little girl scolded, anxious to make sure the little girl's behavior was ever beyond reproach. So the little girl tried hard to please and never to bring shame on herself. It was an unspeakable horror, this dreaded specter named shame. *So good,* the little girl determined to be. And to press the wickedness and the hate and the fear and the aloneness and, most of all, the cry for help from the inadmissible emotions, and the expression of the pain brought on by her seeming helplessness in her dilemma, deep within herself—where no one, not even she herself—would know they still lurked. But an uninvited guest, the shame she evaded, followed the secret occupants into their hidden recesses and stood guard at the gateway lest they plot an untimely escape.

Not until the little girl grew up did she banish all the uninvited and unwelcome intruders from their long-entrenched positions, and when she brought them from their dungeon out into the light, discovered they were but ineffectual shadows there, simply left behind by stepping out into the sunlight.

All her life, from that time on, she felt a special sensitivity for those abandoned children whose life experience somehow skipped over the extension of the warm contact touching the inner recesses of their private dungeons. Her work was not outreach, but *in*-reach, and she knew what it took to look into the darkest recesses and free the sentry to open the heavy gates and bring the specters out into the light that exposed their foolish frailty.

It was her healing work of herself, that she now offered as her gift to others. It's OK to hate, and to rage, little girl, when you've been hurt. Please tell me what you feel. What would help to make it better? What is it you really want and need? I want to know. I want to listen. I will hear you—you are not alone. Your feelings have been felt before, and in sharing them, you will know yourself what to do. Come out of your private hell—I am here for you.

''What is it in me that's too fearsome for your presence to be there? Can you love me, even knowing I sometimes hate you? Please, love me. Please ask to understand me. Please leave yourself and your busy concerns for a few moments to invite me inside to be known. Oh, you are too afraid—it is *you* who dreads being known, not the suspect villain in me? Then let us talk of our villains—can yours be so much worse than mine?

''Please, tell me—out loud, in real words, that I am wonderful. That I can be among the best in this world. That you really know I deserve no shame. That it's OK with you if I'm not always perfect. If I am clumsy, or self-conscious, or shy, or disobedient, or even furious sometimes. Tell me you understand, that you've been there too. Allow me to grow in your trustful acceptance, not in your doubtful haste to condemn. Know that I am good at heart, that I am learning perfectly, that I will turn out to be wonderful and you don't need to be afraid for—or of—me.

"Reach out to me. I wanted to reach out, but my feeble attempts were rebuffed. Know that, and help me find the skill to make the contact. In your heart, you know we're both OK. It's OK just to love."

I hear you. I do love you. Please be safe with me. Share with me all you felt compelled to hide before. There's nothing, no part of you, that I do not love and accept. You are wonderful, a perfect creation unfolding perfectly, and I welcome and bless your process just as it is. It is a constant wonder to me—miraculous, and I thank God for you. My beautiful, beautiful child.

When the writer read this work out loud in journaling class, she looked up with gratitude and told everyone, "The sense of longing for something I needed that was hopelessly unattainable is now gone. What was missing for so long has at last been found. I have given myself what I needed. I feel deeply peaceful inside." When secret feelings from the past are out in the open, the healing can occur.

I recommend writing out the anger, hurt and heartbreak from the past, allowing yourself to *feel* the full range of emotions as you work toward understanding and resolution. Your *Feedback Statement* can often crystallize the learning and act as a catalyst for new action, or a new way of being, that will help to heal the past.

Through Pain and into Joy

I feel the pain that has been buried in me for decades. The part of me that I keep safe and that keeps me dull. I want to grow and feel the heights of joy. Do I have to feel this pain so deeply to do that? Is this what they mean by "going *through* the pain?"

I have carefully avoided pain all my life. I am an expert at avoiding the real pain. I have created a fantasy around me until nothing was real. I created a relationship with someone who would tell me exactly what I wanted to hear. No wonder he left me! I have wanted to live in a dream world, all safe and easy. No pain.

Through pain and into joy
Up the mountain, into the sky
We fly high

Up, up until we meet
The king and queen of deceit
At the point of no return
The sky is blue. I yearn
For truth and freshness
Love and light
From God who makes
My nighttime bright.
Feedback: This *is* going through the pain. Let it go, and choose joy!

What is healthy and joyful for us is always a recurring choice.

I Must Remember

I came very close, so close it scares me, to making myself ill again. My time being stationed in Munich was not easy, and then came the orders here. It was almost as if all I had gained had been lost. Well, a few hours before we were to host a big reception here at our quarters, my back "locked." I had not felt such acute pain since those terrible first months in Maryland. With medication, I got through the three hours. Then the next morning I woke with pain in the area of my left ribs. Somehow I made it through that day, too. I was "entertaining" a visiting V.I.P.'s wife.

Finally, late that afternoon, my awareness began to return. I cleared my schedule and made arrangements to be totally alone for the next two days. These days I spent mostly sleeping, although I did read a little and listen to some quiet, restful music. This morning I woke early, *ready* to get up! I haven't felt like this in a LONG time—truly refreshed, in body, mind, and spirit.

And this is what came out in my writing this morning: I must remember I do not need an excuse for not doing things. All I have to do is say No! I do not *need* to become ill to get out of doing what I don't want to do. That has been my "out" all my life—well, NO MORE!

When I don't stand up for ME, my body does it by becoming ill. Something within me knows what I need. Well, it is time to

change that! I did change in Munich—I helped my SELF to heal—
and I will do so again.

Getting the words out, and then reading them—especially reading them out loud, has magical healing powers. The body no longer
has to store feelings from the past as stress and physical discomfort.

In allowing my emotions to be released through journaling, I have
cried and cried and cried. I found out, however, that writing cleanses
you. It washes out the pain and dark shadows of your soul. It took me
several years of writing about the past until one day, I felt complete
with it, and I shifted to the question: "What did I learn today that will
help me out tomorrow?" I began using my journaling from the present
moment to move forward. Since I have decided to choose joy, I have
really come to understand that journaling is for *joy*.

TURNING POINTS IN YOUR LIFE

The major life decisions you made at significant moments in your
past are still in effect, often subconsciously, today. We may not even
have been aware that we made such a decision at the time, although
we are continuing to live by it today. The following writer realized this
when she wrote about breaking off a long-term comfortable relationship to go with a new boy she had met in college.

You'd Better Not Just 'Think'

"You'd better not just *think* you're in love." I can still hear
Bill saying those words, when I came home and broke the news of
my engagement to someone else. Was he angry? Why didn't he
fight? As I think about this event so long ago, the emotion is surprisingly alive still. The sadness of an unfulfilled relationship—an
incomplete that was never completed. The loss of those dreams
of what could have been.

How different my life might have been if I'd changed my direction on that day! The question had been raised—if I'd only heard
it, instead of charging ahead on blind faith and emotional impulse.

There's so much I could have learned, if I had been awake to Bill's question that day. By *not* paying attention, I made a decision that created a whole different life for me. Too bad I never realized this until after the fact.

Feedback: What this is telling me today is to be very sure of my path. It's not really smart to *sort of* choose or "think" I know. To *know* is so much better.

This was a potentially life-changing moment whose value was allowed to slip by unnoticed at the time. In recalling it years later, the writer has become aware of the importance of conscious choice in her life. As you reflect on your past experience and write about the critical incidents, you may find that you are suddenly aware of the impact certain decisions and choices made on your life.

Decisions I May Have Made as a Small Child

Don't play jacks on an incline!

After being told many times I was "not using my head," I decided that I was not smart.

Doing as I was told made the people in charge happy.

It was more important to make the people in charge happy than to make myself happy.

If I put myself last, others would call on me to do things for them (use me, in a way), and that would make me feel needed and important.

If I smiled a lot, my sister wouldn't bother me about not smiling.

Once when I was five, I decided after being told to clean my part of our room, that if I screamed and cried and threw my sister's stuff at the mirror, someone would finally talk to me.

Feedback: My natural urge to have fun was suppressed by being around so many dysfunctional people as a child. And I've still kept trying to please those people, by keeping up the false facade. Those people will *never* be pleased, and it has nothing to do with me! I don't have to try to please them anymore. I want to be happy now—I *choose* to be happy, and to be around people who are happy. It's OK to have fun.

Once you clearly realize what old attitudes and decisions you have lived your life by, you then have the freedom to make choices that will change your life for the better.

The writer of the next piece recalled from memory a visual impression of a scene which led her as a child to assume that things and people naturally depend on each other for support. This decision relieved her of the requirement to be totally self-sufficient, and confirmed her sense of identity and connection with the natural ways of the world.

It's Natural to Be Supported

In my memory of the orchard, my Uncle Harold stands out amazingly clearly. I see the orchard with its trees laden with fruit so heavy that support braces are need to prop up the branches. I realize that I am like the fruit trees—full, and needing support. Uncle Harold is supported by a chair, the tree limbs are supported by stakes—it's natural for things to be supported in our world, I think. We don't go around floating in thin air!

What decisions have you made in your life? Begin by writing a list of events that stand out in your memory. Let one of these "choose you," or pick one you feel has potential value in exploring. Close your eyes to get a full perceptual sense of the visual and sensory details. Where are you? What are you wearing? What lighting or shadows do you see? What sounds can be heard? What do you smell? Describe your body and how it is reacting. Who else is there? What expressions lighten or darken their faces? What do you imagine they might be thinking? What is said? How is this different from or typical of other scenes in that period of your life? What is assumed and goes unquestioned?

You can further ask yourself: What conclusion or learning did I draw from the incident when it happened? How has the conclusion affected my life? Is it still a valid conclusion to keep today? When you finish writing, give yourself a *Feedback Statement* summarizing your learning.

The Bedroom I Grew Up In

The starkness of the room was startling. Its furnishings were barely adequate. The wood floors were cold, and the metal bed frame stung icily whenever I brushed against it. My bed was pushed tightly against the wall. (No wonder I need freedom today!)

I had just taken an object from its hiding place. It was the crystal-like glass container in which I kept the cigarettes I smoked, secretly, late at night. As I held this object, it became a reminder of my power to make my own decisions. No one can tell *me* what I can and can't do, I thought defiantly, taking a deep drag and inhaling as much of the lung-blackening smoke as I possibly could.

Feedback: Defiance was my defense of last recourse over a rigidly controlled environment. In my anger, I was willing to hurt my own body just to defy my parents' authority. Today, I have beautiful things in my life. I have softness and ruffles and warmth. I have fine things because I deserve them and I am worthy of them. Am I still defying my parents? If so, at least I know I am no longer hurting myself.

Picking an old familiar place, like the home you grew up in and old familiar objects like the pajamas, swimsuit, or tattered shoes you loved; a familiar occasion, like a family holiday or the first day of school; or a particular person out of your past with whom a memory is associated, will help get you into the details stashed away in your memory bank. It will also open up a treasure chest of related recollections and learning.

UNDERSTANDING THE PRESENT BY REMEMBERING THE PAST

Rachel was a thirty-five-year-old woman who wanted to express herself creatively but had never followed through on this desire. She knew she had an artistic gift, and she asked herself, "Why have I never developed my talent before? Why do I lack confidence in this area? Why have I limited myself? What was missing, in my past? When she wrote about these questions in her journal, she recalled several situations when, as a child, her parents had been too busy to give her much encouragement, and she had been too shy and reserved to persist.

We talked of an artist we knew who had a different story: When she was in fourth grade, she painted a mural. Her teacher said to her, "You are an artist." And she told her parents, "This child is an artist. Make sure her talent is developed." Her parents immediately bought art materials for her and she started taking art lessons.

On hearing this story, Rachel said wistfully, "I sure wish someone had done that for *me*."

"In journaling, you have the opportunity to do just that for yourself," I replied, "by understanding what was missing and bringing it back into your life through writing."

Rather than continuing to linger over past choices, and regrets, Rachel set out to resolve them in the present. She thought of further questions to write about: What do I need to do to recover my confidence? In what areas can I express myself more fully now? How can I use my artistic talent? She was determined to give to herself the reinforcement she had longed for all her life, and the acknowledgment of her talent.

Out of the learning she received from her journal, Rachel went on to take art classes. She later wrote and illustrated a children's book. Her art brings her great joy, and she is empowered by people's enthusiastic response to her work.

The following journaling excerpt shows how another woman traced her poor body image and overweight condition to specific experiences in her childhood.

Trust My Own Judgment

I learned at an early age to use food to nurture and protect myself. I remember, as young as six, being aware of weight and thinking I was fat. I was the most self-conscious about my heavy legs. (I have been "sitting on my power" for years, and my legs show it.) At ten my softball coach said I had legs like a piano. I had an image of my legs being huge. Later, when I looked at a picture of myself at thirteen, I realized I had not been fat then at all. Yet by that time I had completely given my power away and was well on the road to becoming fat because of the decisions I had made.

I look back with regret that I didn't see myself accurately. Have I ever? I ask myself now.

Feedback: I have given my power away for such a long time. It is time to trust my own ability to judge myself.

Another journaler gained great insight into understanding a particular behavior pattern and fear by examining her past.

Times I've Been Ignored

Lily came into this world as a peaceful, happy baby, and at an early age learned that being quiet and invisible without complaining was a good way to get love and praise from her mother. Lily found it fairly easy to be invisible as a kid. But on the other hand, she was a pro at stirring the pot, so when being invisible got boring she would go to the other extreme and cause some agitation.

The problem she created for herself was that the more she pretended to be invisible, the more she progressively *became* more and more invisible. As she got older, she found that no one noticed what her needs were, and she had never developed very good skills at expressing them. Even when events came up that were important in her life, no one noticed. Everyone assumed Lily was so "well adjusted." Throughout her childhood and young adult years, no one noticed that Lily too wanted recognition. She had never asked for it. How could she?—everyone was so busy. So Lily got ignored.

Feedback: No wonder I have a fear of no one showing up at my parties! Stop pretending you have no needs, and start asking. People would probably feel good about being able to give to you!

THE MANY DIMENSIONS SHAPING MY STORY

Why is it that some people live through crippling life experiences and come out on the other side strong and sure, while others are scarred all their lives? I know a very successful woman who was terribly abused as a child, and at sixty years old her life was still about denying and disproving that. Journaling opened up a relief valve to let out the tremendous pain she had been holding deep inside all those years.

When she first began journaling about her past, she moved slowly and deliberately, hesitating at each step. But with each approach to peek into her past and see it as it was, the darkness began to lift. Her painful arthritis diminished. She began to see the power of her past as a gift she could now give away to others. Her writing turned into a book in which she shared with the world the powerful lessons her life taught her.

If we look at life through a porthole only wide enough to see what has gone wrong, our life will be a lot different than if we walk right out onto the deck. If we focus on a single subject, we can get a clear picture of that one subject. But if we add a wide-angle lens, we can view a much broader picture. The whole picture is who we are. Why limit our self-perspective to a narrow focus? When you broaden your view, you can benefit from every aspect of your experience.

Look at yourself as a small child. What would others say about you? What would your kindergarten teacher say? How about each grandparent, your mother, father, brother, sister, aunt, uncle, coach, next-door neighbor?

When you were a child, whose primary influence shaped you? Does one person come to mind? How many others can you recall? What new dimensions are there to discover?

Writing about yourself as seen through another person's eyes is very broadening, not only for seeing yourself in a new light, but also in understanding how others related to you. It gets you to "walk a mile in another person's moccasins." The pathway is the same pathway, but somehow different. This is a technique that teaches you to become your own counselor.

A good place to begin is by making a list: People Who Participated in My Childhood Story. One journaler found that her kindergarten teacher stood out in her mind. She decided to write about an early memory from her teacher's point of view.

Hard Lesson for the Headstrong

You get some pretty headstrong ones, in this class. Some who haven't yet figured out who's in charge. They're not used to the routine of a classroom when they come to school for the first time, and they don't realize they have to do what the teacher instructs. You have to show the ones like that that you're the one in authority. Otherwise, the class would be constantly disrupted. It takes a firm hand to bring discipline into the lives of the unruly ones and set the example of how students are expected to behave in class.

Why, I remember one little girl—this kid was determined to finish sawing and painting her cutout wooden teddy bear one day. When it was time to move on to the next activity, she flatly refused. It wasn't fair, she protested. She hadn't gotten her turn at the saw until too late. When I insisted she stop, she got so mad that she tried to grab her coat out of the cloak closet and announced that she was going home right then and there!

There was nothing to do but forcefully restrain her. Kids can't just leave school in the middle of the day. Well, she practically had a tantrum right in the middle of the class. Her big eyes filled with tears of fury, and I could tell she was embarrassed to be crying and humiliated in front of all the other children.

Kids like that never can see how they bring it all on themselves. I don't know why some kids have to make things so hard on themselves. If they'd just do what they're supposed to do in the first place! Learning to mind is a hard lesson for the really stubborn ones.

She blamed *me* for the whole thing, of course. After that day, she lowered her eyes and glowered around me. Though she was subdued from then on, I know she never forgot it. I became an enemy she submitted to with resentment and resistance. As if no matter how nice I tried to be to the class, *she* knew what damage I was capable of doing.

Smart student she was, too. Too smart for her own good, I'd say. Well, I guess she learned her lesson that day. You don't mess with the big guys. If you try it, you'll be sorry. That's what I hate about teaching—when you run up against an obstinate one like that. You can't just teach—it becomes a struggle.

I know she was glad to get out of my class. Even years afterward, she avoided me and never came near the kindergarten classroom. But occasionally I would notice her lingering around the rabbit hutch outside, wishing she were free to come over and pet the bunnies. Serves her right, I'd say.

Feedback: I wonder if Miss Moore really was as spiteful and controlling and insecure as I have pictured her in my skewed memory. This was my first run-in with authority, and my conclusions were far-reaching ones: to accede grudgingly to authority while keeping my real thoughts to myself. Try to get what you want less visibly. People who say what they want and show anger get stomped on, I decided. Rules are more important than people —than me, specifically. And showing your feelings in public is terribly humiliating. Runaway feelings can take a situation out of control.

I saw myself as a victim, not as having provoked this incident. Yet rather than complete surrender, I decided to go underground —strong-willed, yes. I also suspected I was somehow different; no one else in the class ever did such a thing.

These conclusions reinforced my tendencies to keep my feelings in, suppress my emotions, and avoid being direct about what I feel and what I want. They also lowered my self-esteem while preserving a flimsy facade of pride. I made myself invisible to authority figures and suppressed both my weaknesses *and* my strengths for many years. I withdrew and internalized and felt more and more different.

How much of this influence remains today? That's the question. What I will do next is begin keeping a log of times I do and do not express what I feel and want. And I will write how I appreciate what I have learned from this experience and from writing about it.

Like this journaler discovered, the people who inhabit your stored-away memories can reveal important information and truths necessary to your personal healing and joy.

THE LIFE YOU WANT TO BE LIVING

"I wake up every morning with the feeling that I'm not living the life I want to be living. The feelings I want to have are just not there. Something is missing." People often present this complaint, which offers another prime opportunity for journaling. If this issue speaks to you, you might want to try writing about a time in your past when you *were* experiencing the feelings you want to have more of now.

The Time of Tarzan and Jane in My Life

It was a morning like so many other mornings. Mom came into my bedroom and asked, "What do you want for breakfast this morning?" Of course I said, "Pancakes, like always—silver dollar size with lots of butter and syrup." As I lingered in bed, delicious smells soon pervaded the house, and by time I hopped up, there was a stack all ready to eat. Oh, how I loved pancakes (and still do)!

Finishing up an ice-cold glass of milk, I said, "Bye, Mom. I'm going to play with Alan." Out I shot, letting the screen door slam loudly and jumping from the top step to the bottom. I squeezed through the hole between the garage and the fence and cut down through the alley to the Willises' house.

Everyone was in their kitchen when I knocked. Mrs. Willis smiled and invited me in. She always looked like she worked so hard—I guess that's because she did! I asked if Alan wanted to play; I don't think he *ever* said no.

We took off back to my yard, climbing up the fence onto the chicken coop, then up into our "jungle house." Whenever we climbed up on top of the chicken coop, I became Jane and Alan was Tarzan. We would scream back and forth to one another and have a wonderful time. Facing the gravest of dangers, we would always figure some way to survive.

Oh, the hours, days, years I spent in fantasy, having a wonderful, carefree time. That was living each and every day to the fullest.

Feedback: After reading this over, I realize how important play is in children's lives. Piaget said play is a child's work. I am

naturally a player and am excited about keeping that part of me
TOTALLY ALIVE.

This is a wonderful opportunity for you to stretch back into your
memory. Remember the first time you tasted ice cream. Recall a childhood friend with whom you played—what were your favorite games?
Did you like to pretend? Was there a relative with whom you shared
special times?

Another journaler returned to the hectic but happy times of her
early married life for insight into what was missing and what she
needed more of in her life today.

Going Home

I want to go home! Where is home? I want to go home to my
female self. Sometimes it looks like the house in Logan Bay, bak-
ing cookies in my colorful kitchen, kids tromping in and out. Sewing
new dresses for the girls, going to parents' night at school. Watching Eva and her friends play volleyball, basketball, and softball. Going
to all her games. Taking classes at Bianca and enjoying the intellectual stimulation. Going to Kingston Village with my girlfriends, talking and laughing all night. All the wonderful conversations about
ghosts and reincarnation. Fourth of July picnics in Jed's backyard.
Making love with Ken in the woods in the Serena foothills. Bike
riding every evening with Ken, the kids in baskets on the front and
back of our bikes. Picking ripe apricots and canning them at the
cannery; making strawberry jam and plum cobbler. Feeding the
ducks at the park—oh, how the kids loved to feed the ducks!

Christmas family night at church, making decorations, watching
the kids perform in the nativity, eating hot dogs. Walking down
the street in our neighborhood after the rain, with the mountains
so clear at the end of the street and a rainbow overhead. Driving
to Valera Bend for apples and cider and just sitting by the river,
watching the water rush over the rocks. Ken, rolling on the floor
with all the kids on top of him laughing and yelling. Birthday parties for each child's birthday with all the neighborhood kids. Sitting in the backyard reading my homework and listening to the

birds. Picking bouquets of roses from the garden and filling vases with them, smelling the wonderful fragrance all over the house. Justin bringing me a flower every day. Eva getting up at six o'clock to go to practice, and Lickens playing with Marianne and Sophie. Tiger Tom sneaking up on the table to bask in the sun when I wasn't home and jumping down when he saw my car pull up.

Walking on the beach at sunset with Ken, feeling so close and wonderful. Dinners at the Blue Ox Inn, laughing and joking with friends. Endless loads of wash and ironing spilling out of baskets. Putting out toys on Christmas Eve after the kids went to bed. Going to the airport to meet Ken for lunch. Ken's calling me every day, and I thought he was checking up on me, but he just wanted to talk. Ruthie playing her guitar and singing, going skiing with Tony and Lynn. Eating chocolate cream pie from Pete's Pie Shop.

Even then, I needed more balance. I needed a man I could talk to on the same intellectual and spiritual level. God bless the good things from that life. I was very much in my feminine self. As a single woman I have been too much in my masculine side. I want balance more today than ever before.

Now is the time for a new nest, a relationship, new experience, new home, new balance and red roses! In those days I had to keep going to survive, to take care of the kids. I didn't have time to fully grieve, so my grief showed up in my body. I was always keeping myself busy, going somewhere, so I wouldn't have to feel the pain, the grief, the loneliness, the sadness. Now the kids are off on their own and I'm letting myself feel it all so I can let it go. My next experience will be fresh and brand-new.

Douchan Gersi, the explorer, talked about living in the moment, cherishing every little thing, seeing how precious our earth is and how precious our relationships are. I do not need to go to Borneo to realize the sacredness of life,

As you learn to draw on the strength of powerful and positive memories you will gain the ability to make life-affirming choices, particularly the ones that bring joy. The life you want to be living is based on a decision to live the life you choose—given the choice, why not choose joy!

I remember my grandmother once finding an old trunk in the attic and telling me stories about the memories associated with the old clothes she discovered there. I expected her to place everything carefully back inside afterwards. She did not, and in fact, she threw them away and set the trunk outside in the sunlight to air out. I realized that she didn't want anyone to be burdened with having to dispose of her old memories. Only a few special things were kept.

The same logic applies when you air out your trunk of old memories. You hold them up to the light, examine and sort through, and keep only those that have value, meaning, and use for you now.

Life is a great adventure. By opening up the album of stored memories, you allow yourself to re-create, rethink, and recapture the valuable thoughts and precious feelings you may have missed somewhere along the way.

4

Listing Your Life

ALITTLE GIRL wants a jump rope buried underneath all the playground equipment: she has to dump the box out to find it. The game can't be played if the needed equipment is lost in a tangled mess of nets and balls.

It's hard to journal meaningfully if your mind looks like the inside of that playground box. The first step is to dump out the disarray and get everything out where you can see it. Then you can tell what you have, and maybe put the items back in organized positions, so you can get at them more easily next time.

Writing a list is a simple way of dumping out the toy box in your mind. Often, you find things you had long forgotten were there, like the delighted child stopping to play with each newly discovered treasure. "Dumping out" your disorder onto paper places the multitude of ideas, concerns, solutions and action steps where you can sort them and make use of them. More than mulling things over in your mind or even talking them out, order and action often come from the concrete process of writing them down. Organizing your thoughts on paper gives you a means of taking charge of your life.

Lists are an extremely valuable tool for organizing large amounts of scattered information into orderly, manageable batches—thus freeing the mind to focus at any one point. Lists are great for identifying patterns in your life, too.

The examples in this chapter model many ways of using lists. As you go through and try some of the exercises yourself, you may want to *make a list* of other ideas and future journal writing topics that pop into your head. A list can always lead you to your next journaling step or assignment.

The most commonly used kind of list is what I call the "mind-cleaning" list. It replaces the act of holding onto all sorts of information in your head. You jot down lists of things to do, groceries needed, people to call, items to shop for, bills to pay, letters to write, books to read, homework assignments to complete, errands to run. These lists are quickly done and free up your energy. Often they effectively remove the feelings of procrastination and the vague apprehension accompanying disorganized thoughts.

Jobs to Ask Jeff to Help With

Mount poles in closet
Replace window parts
Paint the fence or get someone to do it
Reinforce railing around the deck
Hang pictures
Transplant begonias
     Feedback: Jeff can handle all this easily—give the list to him tomorrow.

The list that evolves for you will often point out the way toward needed action. Lists lend themselves well to creative manipulation, so take a second look at yours. Do you want to organize items, put them into categories or assign priorities? If you make an action plan, how about a schedule with specific dates?

WHAT BRINGS ME JOY

Joy, our desired state, is also our natural state. But a lot of confusion and interference can get between us and our natural state of joy. Sometimes we become so comfortable and used to feeling confused and blocked that these states seem more natural to us than the state of joy. We walk around under a dark cloud of doom, instead of walking around under a rainbow. One of the most important lists you can make—and keep making often, because it will tend to change constantly—is a list of *what brings you joy.*

What Brings Me Joy

The sounds and smells of the ocean
Watching my children when they sleep
Listening to beautiful music
Knowing I've done a good job
Opening an envelope with money
Stepping on the scale and seeing my perfect weight
Catching a shooting star
The adventure of traveling to new places
The ecstasy of eating a truffle
Spending time in art galleries and museums
A romantic dinner
> *Feedback:* These things and many more make my heart sing.

This kind of writing prepares you to be joyful. It reminds you to make joy a priority. It reminds you to come from the positive rather than the negative. It strengthens you in the face of events that might overwhem you. When you have pages of joy lists in your journal, you can be with them, reread them and renew them any time you choose.

I worked with a teenage girl whose dilemma was whether or not to apply for college and what to do with her life. When I asked what her special talents and gifts were, she could identify only, "Certainly not math." She had been so preoccupied with her weaknesses, including what was *wrong* with her and what she disliked that answering the question of what brought her joy felt like speaking a foreign language.

As we focused in on what she was best at, what was natural for her, what felt good, Becky realized that she was naturally good at working with people in a leadership role and was curious about science. Once we had compiled a quick list of what she loved to do, this young woman was prepared to base her life decisions on talents, gifts and what she wanted, rather than on what she didn't want to do—or wasn't good at.

What you *know* is what you *are*. Once you identify what experiences and conditions bring you satisfaction and joy, you will have the information to make your moment-to-moment and major life decisions.

WHO AM I?

I was at a seminar once when a man came up to me and asked, "Who are you?" I pointed to my name tag and said, "I'm Joyce."

"Yes," he said—"and who are you?"

"I'm Joyce Chapman," I replied, giving a little more information I thought he must be probing for.

"Yes, but *who are you?*" he asked again, with a playful smile in his inquisitive eyes.

"I've been invited to this seminar because I like to learn about these kinds of things."

"Yes, but who are you?" I was beginning to catch onto the game now, so I skipped the expected responses like what my job was, who I knew, and who I was related to. Finally, I arrived at: "I'm a joyful person who came to light up the room."

"Yes, and you are so much more too. Now, who are you?"

I laughed about this encounter for a long time. When I finally arrived at the bottom line of who I am, I got to the heart of the matter—the joy. But there were so many labels and outer definitions to get through first.

How very important it is to know *who we are!* And how few of us contemplate it, or delve into this important subject. In some of my classes, we do an exercise in which we write a list every day for a year titled *Who Am I?* The writing changes from day to day and over time provides an unfolding self-portrait that is powerfully revealing.

Who Am I

I love to stand on mountaintops
I love to play
I am a fabulous cook and love good food
I am the son of a remarkable person
Others can count on me
I take responsibility for my actions
I am committed to my best physical presentation
I am a wisdom seeker on a spiritual path
    Feedback: This is good . . . I'm growing.

Write as many ways of defining and explaining yourself as you can think of. This is a great way to strengthen your sense of self. It forces you to be congruent when you start honing in on a clear definition of who you are—and writing it down. This can be followed with a second list, *Who Do I Want to Be?*, with a *Feedback Statement* comparing the two lists and concluding what action or changes they suggest.

WHAT I WANT

There is power in knowing your own mind. I once taught a course called "Your Life Is Your Choice," in which each session opened with an exercise of writing a *What I Want* list without editing, ranking or prioritizing.

What I Want

To be loved by my husband
To be appreciated by my boss
To sing more
To laugh more
To eat peanut butter by the spoonful
To be as joyful as the teacher
To make these kinds of lists that move me to where I want to be in life.
    Feedback: This may work!

Every area of our lives is affected by knowing intimately what we want. It's very refreshing to be around people who know what they want. Writing a *What I Want* list can set your desires into motion.

I often observe, however, a lot of resistance to writing these kinds of lists. Such issues come up as: Will I be tied down to doing something specific to get what I want? Will I be forced to make some changes? Will I become disillisioned if I write and what I want doesn't magically appear? Will I become self-centered and egotistical? Will I insist on having what I want at everyone else's expense? Will that little sheet of paper take me by the collar and force me to become someone I don't want to be?

What I have experienced is that a person who identifies what they want and is willing to commit to the action to get it, is also one who is reaching for their full potential. Making a list is the first—and essential step. It plants the seed and the subsequent action follows it through.

What I also have found is that when people delve deeply enough into what they want, they find it's not, ultimately, about power, riches and fame. What they really want is love, fulfillment and self-expression. Many realize that one of the greatest joys is giving their gift to others. Having what we want is closely tied to serving others, and helping others receive what *they* want. Writing—and discovering—what you want is the powerful first step, but not more than that.

In writing *What I Want* lists, you often find yourself writing a parallel *What I Don't Want* list. The "what I wants" become clearer in contrast to the "don't wants." I know a person who decided to rent out rooms in her large house. At first she tried to foresee any problems that might arise: "I certainly don't want anyone who uses drugs, drinks, or smokes, makes a lot of noise, or entertains undesirable friends. I also don't want anyone I have to clean up after—no one messy. And I don't want to have to beg people to pay the rent on time." From these ideas she created a very clear list of the qualities she was looking for in selecting people to share her house with.

What I'm Looking for in a Renter

Someone I can trust completely
Someone who will always pay the rent on time
An employed, responsible person
Someone respectful of the house and property
A clean, neat, organized person who will share the housework
Someone who doesn't smoke, drink, or do drugs
Someone who appreciates and gets along well with my child

Each time her renters turned over, new concerns arose bringing up new things to think about. She added to and revised the list many times.

Additional Qualities I'm Looking for in Renters

Considerate of others
Willing to recognize that they are not the ones running the show
Works regularly and gone during the day, usually
Not a college kid with phone calls coming in every minute
Used to the responsibilities of living independently, not looking for
a mother
Healthy, not sickly
Never using supplies or food that belong to others

It took over a year before this woman had developed a clear enough idea of what she wanted and could put it in the form of a written rental contract. Finally, she got so clear that she summed up all her requirements up in a single sentence: "I want the person I select to be more of an asset than a liability to everyone." Defining "What I Want" is an evolving process. It can be a very beneficial and rewarding one in both the short and long term.

MILESTONES IN YOUR LIFE

Ira Progoff in his authoritative work called *AT A JOURNAL WORKSHOP* introduces the concept of *steppingstones* as a way of gaining an overall perspective on an individual's life. Steppingstones are turning points or significant events that mark and change your life.

Milestones of My Life So Far

Going fishing all summer long the year I was seven
Deciding to like school when I was ten
Winning the championship spelling bee in junior high
Making the cheerleader team
Standing in Miriam's living room as she hemmed up my formal
The day I left home to go to college
Getting my first job in film production
My wedding day
Joining Alcoholics Anonymous and staying sober!

Writing a list like this one can easily lead to ideas for further exploration and journaling. You could write a paragraph or piece on each milestone, or turn each one into a chapter in the book called *My Life Story*.

You can also look at your list and ask yourself: what was the decision I made from each milestone—about myself, about others, or about the way the world is? Write a *Feedback Statement* beginning, "Out of these experiences I learned . . ."

The writer of the preceding list noted that her milestones all marked points of great change in her life. "I learned that every choice has the potential of changing the entire course of my life, even if it seems small and insignificant at the time," she said.

In thinking about the advantages of writing your milestones, you can identify:

- stages

- progressions

- learnings

- decisions

- inspirations

- wishes & dreams

- successes

- failures

There are also more kinds of milestones to list: development of your self-esteem; declaration of your independence; forming your sexual identity; recovering from addiction; or creating healthy and happy relationships.

Audrey was an older woman who came into my office saying, "I hate my life. I go from one person's demands to another. Not a minute of my time can I really call my own. It's nothing more than a contemporary form of slavery—and there is no escaping all these perfectly rational demands."

I invited her to make a list of the milestones of her independence and the actions she took toward personal freedom during the course of her life.

Milestones of Freedom

1. Choosing a hairstyle nobody liked—but I did
2. Painting my bedroom black and red
3. The day I told my Dad I *was* going out with Frank, whether he liked it or not
4. Sitting on the plane on my way to college when I realized that my mom—not me—had made the choice of where I would go, and had made most of my choices up to that time. Deciding I was in charge from then on
5. The day I stayed home from work and slept all day not because I was sick, but because I needed to
6. Changing my religion, at the expense of my family's condemnation
7. The years I demonstrated for women's rights and ventured into "unsafe" areas
8. Thinking that being married would set me free and then that day I spent alone deciding I was not free, wondering if I could be free and be married at the same time
9. The day I realized that Paul never asks me permission to go out running—why do I feel I have to ask him for permission to go see a friend?
10. Realizing—at age 40!—that it was time to stop believing that "Daddy (or my husband, boss, etc.) will make it better," and to start taking care of myself
11. Telling my husband I *was* going to take that expensive class that we couldn't afford, and I would find a way to pay for it
12. Discovering my journal can set me free by letting my secrets go and by reflecting, learning, and choosing what I want to do

Feedback: Freedom is a daily *choice* with big consequences. It's a choice I have been able to make many times in the past, and can make now. Put CHOOSE FREEDOM on an affirmation card and remember it!

Audrey realized that she had been dealing with the issues of autonomy and self-assertion for much of her life. This journal exercise not only helped her to get in contact with the times she succeeded in making her own decisions and being her own person, but also the realization that personal freedom was her responsibility and under her conscious control.

MY BELIEFS

What do you believe? Start with the most basic areas of your life. "What do I believe about . . . my family, friendships, health, relationships, money, higher power? Out of that journaling, an abundance of stored information from which to examine your beliefs will unfold. By examining your belief system you start to identify what your beliefs about every aspect of your life really are. Look at your old beliefs to see which ones were yours that you no longer need or want, or more importantly, which ones are the beliefs someone else gave you that you no longer believe. The examination of your beliefs brings the awareness to change. Only by being clear about your current beliefs can you live your life from choice.

As you become clear about what you believe, you get in touch with the passion of living. When you live from the conviction of your beliefs, then your actions and words take on power and authority.

Your beliefs develop by first being identified, then questioned, tested, changed, refined, or reaffirmed. What do you believe about how you got here? What do you believe about right and wrong? What do you believe is important in life? What do you value? What do you believe about the meaning of life? What do you believe about the nature of the universe? About nature? About childhood? About politics? About God? About the age we live in? What is your purpose in life?

I Believe

In the value of human life
In a loving God who is the source of all good
That I am completely forgiven for any wrongs I have committed

That my destiny is *huge* and I will fulfill it easily
The right people are coming into my life now, and will stay!
I am able to be rich and successful
The universe is an abundant source of supply, and I am tapped into its "bank"
I am an important change agent in the world
I am secure wherever I am
That the aging process can be reversed
That I am an articulate, powerful communicator.

 Feedback: As I read over where I am, I realize that I have come a long, long way.

As a society, we have collected massive information from science, history, the arts, technology, etc., that constantly challenges our belief systems. Defining and redefining our beliefs awakens the sleeping giant inside, because our beliefs are what give us the power to act accordingly.

You might want to be more specific in listing your beliefs, according to the issues you are dealing with in your life right now. You might want to list your beliefs about growing old, death, marriage, sexuality, war, parenting, children, education, religion, politics, or bosses.

All My Beliefs About Money

My father won't understand my need to spend money this way.
Real estate is my main source of income.
I can have anything I want.
See it and you'll have it.
You'll betray your whole family if you move above their income bracket.
It takes too much responsibility to become rich.
You owe it to all the poor people in the world to never have more than they do.
We can't afford that.
That dress is too expensive—let's go find some fabric and make one.
I'd never be able to support myself completely.
I am worth every cent I make and much, much more.

I am highly paid for my services.
Everyone is enriched by my services.
People appreciate my quality services and are happy to pay for the value they receive.

    Feedback: I have a lot of inconsistency and confusion in my beliefs. I have some new beliefs that are being contradicted by old, outdated ones I want to get rid of.

As a follow-up later, I often recommend going back over the list of beliefs and crossing out any that no longer fit who you are today.

Once you have made your own list of beliefs, in order to further examine and understand yourself, try writing on the subject: What are the significant life events that have influenced and formed each of my beliefs?

Life Event	Belief
• being in the nursery with Daisy watching the Wizard of Oz.	• the real babies were much more fun than my baby doll
• jumping off the roof into a pile of snow	• I wasn't afraid—I knew nothing could harm me
• on the stage in high school	• I don't need to be nervous in front of anybody
• went into a grown-up job, with insurance and everything	• I *can* take care of myself
• round-trip ticket to Paris and a modeling contract	• I can do whatever it takes to have what I want

You can constantly be collecting new information to influence and form your beliefs as they are always in a state of flux. Listing your beliefs on paper pins them down for one moment in time. The habit of frequently listing your beliefs connects you with the enthusiasm and aliveness that comes from living in congruence with your convictions.

RECOGNIZING BLOCKS AND PATTERNS

I have found that lists are one of the easiest and fastest ways to uncover our blocks and patterns. Lists can lead us to choosing new patterns of thinking and behaving when we don't like what we see and recognize that the old way is no longer working for us.

Whatever is blocking you from getting what you want can provide the clue for making a list. Ask yourself what list would be the most beneficial to make in your life right now.

A client, Kelly, one day reeled off to me dozens of small incidents where she had "filled in" for her husband's negligence, always telling herself that "It really doesn't matter; it's just a small thing. It's OK that he forgets to call. It's his habit to be an hour or two late—I've gotten used to it. His mother never taught him to clean up after himself, and he still has a hard time with it. I don't think he really meant to hurt me—it was just a slip of the tongue." Then she would go to the bathroom and cry when she hurt, or go to the refrigerator and eat—ignoring the behaviors and hoping he would change someday.

Kelly made a list of all the things she feared: "To tell him I'm relaxing and don't feel like getting up to get him a beer; to tell my step-daughter that if she doesn't get off drugs, she can't come to visit anymore; to tell his parents we're not coming to the picnic." She literally felt that if she told the truth, the roof would cave in. "I have no courage at all," she said, and proceeded to make another list of ways to successfully change her pattern.

Within six months of her commitment to find and discover her needs, Kelly recognized her patterns and began to take the first precarious steps toward total responsibility for her reactions and choices. As she moved forward through the process of telling herself the truth and aligning with what she needed, her lists became smaller and smaller.

Change can come from writing about what seems to be blocking you from being the person you want to be. Any aspect of your life can benefit from the scrutiny a simple list provides. If you are unsatisfied with a relationship, you might think of several lists to write:

- What's troubling you.

- What changes need to be made in the relationship.

- Why you want the relationship.

- What you want from the relationship.

- What you're willing to do for the relationship.

- What you're not willing to do for it.

Another journal writer who was crippled by fear decided, "I don't want to be run by fear anymore. I want to understand it and complete it, and be done with it forever." She made the following list:

What I Fear

What I fear is freezing to death.
What I fear is being raped.
What I fear is Tom leaving me.
What I fear is losing Tom to another woman.
What I fear is the IRS.
What I fear is getting sick and dying.
What I fear is being poor.
What I fear is police harassment.
What I fear is going to Nicaragua.
What I fear is public speaking.
What I fear is being ridiculed.
What I fear is Hell's Angels.
What I fear is being alone.
What I fear is scary people.
What I fear is other people's anger.
What I fear is intimidating people.
What I fear is crying in public.
What I fear is not being good enough.
What I fear is burning in a fire.
What I fear is my own fears.
     Feedback: Most of what I fear is lacking in my life.

Having achieved some very interesting insights, she then made another list:

What I Like

What I like is to be funny.
What I like is to be fearless.
What I like is to eat.
What I like is to not be judgmental.
What I like is to be myself.
What I like is to have friends.
What I like is to be with my dogs.
What I like is to have plenty of money.
What I like is to have my own house.
What I like is to have a clean house.
What I like is cheesecake.
What I like is to feel alive.
What I like is to laugh.
    Feedback: Most of what I like is lacking in my life right now.

When this journaler read back over her lists, she was surprised at the *Feedback Statement* that had emerged. Out of this very powerful writing, she was able to make an important decision: to stop focusing her energy on her fears and start using it to bring more of what she liked into her life. In replacing a new list for the old, she is literally beginning a new way of thinking and acting that will better serve her.

One of the things that happens when you start writing about your life is that the need to make lists arises out of what you have written. The following writer found herself feeling sad about the prospect of getting ready for another Christmas. She honored this feeling and decided to explore it and figure out how to change her experience of Christmas into a more balanced and joyful one.

Christmas Alone

    I was sad last night when I asked Craig to help me put the lights on the Christmas tree and he said no. I'm so tired of having no nurturing. I want someone to help me with the family celebrations. What is it in me that stops this type of loving and sharing from coming into my life?

The clock just chimed. It seems to say, my time is now. Probably what I should notice, instead of getting stuck in the rut of "It's happening again . . ." is the impact of Julia's stating so clearly what she wanted and needed, this past weekend. It was very obvious that she shared some of the same feelings I was having. We are both mostly givers, not receivers.

How can I achieve the balance I need of giving and receiving? If I am to change my pattern, it is important to decide what I want, write it out, communicate, and set *myself up to win*.

Feedback: Make a list to help me sort out what I'm learning here, and how I can change it to experience more joy and fun. I want to *celebrate* the season this year!

From this reflective writing, the following list emerged:

My Learning

1. I want it to be different.
2. Craig is not going to be different—he doesn't care about Christmas preparations.
3. My expectations of Craig are unrealistic.
4. My feelings of being overburdened about Christmas are partly a monster from my past. I have always tended to carry the whole load myself.
5. I have set myself up my whole life to hold the world for everyone else!
6. I am not responsible for the success or failure of everyone else's Christmas.
7. I must nurture myself, and ask for what I need.

After creating this list of very revealing observations, this writer went on to devise ways to move her out of unhappy patterns into forming healthier new ones:

My New Patterns

1. Invite friends and family over to decorate the house.
2. Share honestly with Craig my desire for his participation—and my need to be nurtured.

3. If I want to decorate, then do it for myself, without resentment. If I don't, then skip it.
4. Put myself on my Christmas list—love myself.
   Feedback: Don't forget—I love Christmas!

As a journaler delves yet deeper into self-understanding each time a curious, wonderful or problematic incident arises in daily life, a list may be called out to be written—a list of other similar incidents or similar learnings. These are often accessed easily by using the sentence starter "Times I've . . .".

Writing a list of similar times is a very good way to achieve the kind of "Aha!" that moves you from being "the effect" of your life to being *at cause* in your life events. Once you see the pattern and want to break it, you can look at your list and ask simply, "What do I need to do about this?"

A distraught client came into my office once and said, "I feel like I must be wearing a shirt that says 'I am a scapegoat—kick me.' The computer is malfunctioning, we don't have a printer to do the job, both the department heads want their work done yesterday, this little dog is wandering around all our desks yapping at everyone, and six people are carrying on different phone conversations all at once in our tiny office. I'm trying to hold all this together at once, and my boss comes in, tosses the financial analysis statement from last year on my desk, and says, 'This statement is a year old. Why hasn't it been updated quarterly?' "

Because she wanted to keep her job a little longer, we arrived at a new strategy for coping with the office chaos. Instead of taking every incident as a life-or-death situation, she was to consider her work as a learning lab—preparation or apprenticeship for future, more ideal jobs. She began her education by listing other times in her life when she had seen herself as a scapegoat. Here is part of the list she made:

Times I Was Made a Scapegoat

1. At Simpsons' almost always! I think it was because I was the youngest of the group and the most gullible. I will never forget the time that the operations manager of the whole division blamed me personally for not meeting our quota! I laughed in

his face because I thought he was joking, but he wasn't. He was totally serious. He said I was two days behind in putting the dollars shipped amount on the board for the workers to see, so they didn't know how much to produce! I'd never heard anything so ludicrous in my entire life. Posting production quantities was supposed to be a morale booster, not to take the place of the entire production control department!

2. More again at Simpsons'. I resented it very much that problems were blamed on me because "the message didn't get to the manager on time." . . . Oh, how that used to frustrate me! Luckily, I had a very honest and positive rapport with most of the customers, and they knew when the manager was lying to cover himself. But it still irked me to realize that I had no support from my manager, but plenty of support from my customers. It seemed so backwards!

Feedback: These incidents remind me of how I felt being the youngest of five children. All the adults in my life were so overpowering, I learned to accept being blamed for whatever went wrong. I couldn't speak up for myself then—but I can now!

What a powerful learning experience for this client to move through beliefs that had shaped her life for years, and step into her adult role.

A LIST OF LISTS

The list of lists you can think of to journal on is virtually endless. Here are some additional suggestions to choose from. Run your finger down this list, and stop at the item that catches your attention, or make up your own:

- Things I do well.

- Times I've felt fulfilled.

- Things I love.

- What I like about myself.

- Positive experiences I've had.

- People I like being with.

- Ways I am like my . . . mother, father, teacher, my parents' ideal.

- Excuses I sometimes use.

- Times I've sold out.

- Times I've been acknowledged.

- Times I've been wrong.

- Times I've been right, how I knew it, and what I did.

- Great losses in my life—and what the learning was.

- Times I've been sick or had accidents—What was going on in my life at the time.

- Things I would do if I were the person I admire, left my misery behind and had no excuses.

- Things I need to handle in order to restore my integrity.

- Times I've wanted to quit/give up.

- What I want to add to my life.

- What I want to eliminate from my life.

- Times I've felt creative.

- Things I want to be remembered for.

5

Creative Conversations

W E CAN *TALK* about walking a mile in another person's moccasins, but what if we actually put those moccasins on and set out walking in them? We can try to imagine what another person's experience might be like, but the actual experience is always more real. We can try on a costume, but actually playing a character's role challenges us to be interactive in a real and immediate way. Personal relationships between parts of ourselves and our own conflicting motives are clarified when individuals bump up against each other, assert their intentions, and use every bit of tact and diplomacy to get what they want.

In this chapter, we will explore writing conversations that take you beyond speculating about people, events, and issues into actually *being* the person or event—playing out the part, and speaking the lines. In writing conversations, we discover that we really *do* know the other person's point of view. Even though we haven't experienced it, by discovering their voice through writing, we can access another person's reality.

Ira Progoff once said, "An artist is always in dialogue with his or her work." We are the artists; our creation is our life. By writing conversations, we can be in constant communication or dialogue with our life.

Does your relationship to your life resemble that of a married couple whose communication died nineteen years ago? You know, the kind of relationship that continues on, locked into automatic pilot, in a time-worn routine, out of touch with true desires and wants. Why settle for that? You need not accept the loss of your individuality or *self*. A full and vital life thrives on ongoing interaction and purposeful creation. Our relationship to life can flourish with excitement and enchantment if we keep the communication within ourselves flowing and alive.

CONVERSING WITH YOURSELF

Who knows more about you than you do? Somewhere inside of you is the answer to any question you could ever ask. One great way to tap into your answers is to hold a conversation with yourself. An easy way to do this is to set up a dialogue between "you, the interviewer" and "you, the interviewee." The advantage to using another person (the interviewer) is that it eliminates any self-judgment. Instead of "beating yourself up" you are "bringing yourself up" to become the person you want to be. I often tell people it's like writing a play. You would stage a conversation between you and another character in the same way you would write dialogue for a play.

What if you don't know what one of your characters would say to the other? Make it up! I knew a dancer who had always had a lot of physical problems with her feet. She had no idea that her feet could talk to her—how silly that seemed! But when she wrote a conversation between herself and her feet, an interesting insight emerged: her feet "told" her, "When you start to work on your *soul*, your feet will be OK." Her subconscious mind had made a connection between *sole* and *soul*, and her body had been nagging her to pay more attention to her spiritual well-being!

When a revelation like this emerges, not only is it life-changing, it's a powerful invitation to align with your life's purpose. It led her to a path of spiritual self-discovery and investigation of alternative healing methods. By embracing the evolution of her "soul," she eliminated the chronic physical foot pain within a year.

Often after you have written a piece that connects you with your truth, you may feel that "Maybe I *am* just making it up." The important question here is this: are you learning from it? Your imagination can be a channel for accessing your inner knowing.

Sometimes we are stymied at starting a conversation with ourself. It can often get its start from doing a little pondering and puttering with your pen about what "needs to be written."

Hello, My True Self

If I looked at what I need to get in touch with today, it would be to know what my true self wants to do. What does my life plan say is next for me?

Toni: Hello, True Self. Please come out and talk to me about what's next. There's a new part of me that's ready to surface. I can feel it. It's time, really time, for me to bring forth more of who I am and bring all my parts into alignment.

True Self: Well, the first thing you need to admit is your frustration in staying with a job that is holding you back from reaching your true potential.

Toni: You've got that right. The thought of a career change has crossed my mind, but I guess I have been avoiding making a major decision like that. What do you advise? What is the job that I could be really happy in?

True Self: Are you ready to stop letting others make your decisions for you?

Toni: What's that got to do with it? Oh, I guess I would have to give up Jerry's pressure to succeed and my fear of letting Dad down if I left this job.

True Self: So true. They may not approve of me—they've hardly ever allowed themselves to be creative and spontaneous. It's obvious that they don't trust their own true selves.

Toni: OK, then, I am ready to decide for myself. What do you recommend?

True Self: Let's look at what you need, to be happy expressing your true self. More flexibility in your schedule—that's surely important. And being able to spend lots of time outdoors. The sun and fresh air breathe life into you. You wilt and wither being cooped up in an office. What you'd love most is to show the whole world how to have as much fun as you do on your sailboat, sharing good times with good friends.

Toni: Of course, but I never considered mixing my pleasure with business.

True Self: Oh? . . .

Feedback: Being true to myself means loving what I do. How much happier I will be! I will look further into these new career possibilities.

You can invent countless other ideas for conversations to have with parts of yourself. Perhaps you will want to dialogue between your personal and your professional self. Or start a dialogue with the two-year-old child or the rebellious teenager inside you who now wants more than to be seen and not heard, or with the judgmental rule-maker that resides within you. Extremely valuable is the conversation between the male and female sides of one's personality. Other examples are dialogues between you and the vulnerable and nurturing parts, or your spiritual self. Try a debate between "What I really want to do" versus "What I am willing to do."

One woman felt caught in a bind between the demands of maximizing her potential and the practical realities of paying the bills. She wrote the following revealing conversation with her "Highest Potential."

What Is It Like to Be You?

Those old doubts and fears about being self-employed have surfaced again like shark's fins in troubled water. I want to be guided by my highest potential, not by fear. What is the answer?

Me: So, HP, what is it like to be you?

HP: It is an amazing thing. If you only knew, you would do anything for it.

Me: Maybe so, but that doesn't help me much now.

HP: OK, I'll be more specific. Your life as *me* is: so full of energy that you feel fully nourished by and treated to *life*. Doing what you love, you can't wait to get to it. Your thoughts are high and bright; the future looks promising. Through channeling your creativity, you are fully energized and vitalized. You are one with the world, and life loves to welcome you. You honor your body as your vehicle and take loving care of it.

Me: Sounds appealing—but overly idealistic.

HP: Have you given up hope, then?

Me: I have to face reality, don't you understand? *You* don't have to pay bills and plan for a "secure future." You don't have the temptation to opt out and settle for something safe, secure, and certain. How can I come to terms with that need and still honor my need to be like you?

HP: But have you given up, then?

Me: Well, I must admit I have been leaning that way, in my more depressed moments lately. I've not been feeling well, you know. Wanting to crawl under the covers and hide.

HP: So what's that all about? Have you made your decision but are not willing to face the results of it yet? Are you just putting off the inevitable?

Me: That depends on what day you talk to me. I do have brighter moments. I'm very indecisive, lately. My money situation seems to be speaking out strongly for *some* kind of change, and the world's response to my independence has been disappointing. Whatever new possibilities are there after this job is done are certainly not apparent to me now.

HP: You know, you don't really have to worry about that *now*. If you just put your energy fully into doing *this* job, the new possibilities will be there when the time comes.

Me: Yes, but that hasn't been working out as well as I'd like. I've checked out so many possibilities, and gotten too little response. Who can afford the work I want to do? I want money not to be a problem! Isn't it wiser to have some stable plan for the future?

HP: You know, if you give up now, you may regret it. You may sell out on your courage to dream big again.

Me: Of course, that's why I feel so stuck. I can't give up, yet something has to give.

HP: Remember—Don't give up—give *more*.

Me: I know that's what I will do, for now. I'll be getting into this new project now with all I've got, and leaving all these doubts behind again—another time. I just hope you're right about the possibilities down the road.

HP: You really ought to look at fulfilling some of those parts of yourself you haven't attended to lately. If you made yourself happier, you wouldn't worry so much, you know.

Me: You're right. What's my next move?

HP: Find a group to get involved with, musically and socially. Meet some people, and stop being so down. Take charge.

Me: Let's get back to the question, what about my two conflicting needs?

HP: The answer's simple, of course. Choose the one you want, and both will be taken care of. Nothing can be handled by wavering. All is handled in the choice. It might take more than a year, though. Would you give up after only one year of trying?

Me: Thank you, HP. I will listen to you more often. How come I get so far off track sometimes?

HP: You are just coming to terms with unwise choices of your past. You're still learning, and you want to avoid making unnecessary mistakes again. Listen inside—and write more. *That's where you are me.*

CONVERSING WITH YOUR BODY

It is important to be in constant dialogue with our bodies. Without a body, we don't get to be here. Yet people tend to ignore the non-verbal communications the body continuously sends—until the body turns up the volume louder and louder, and we end up with a scream-ing pain that finally demands our full attention.

When your body claims your attention in some way, be sure to have a conversation with it, listening for the message it wants to com-municate with you. As a matter of routine maintenance and to *max-imize the joy* of being in your body, learn to keep your channels of communication open.

Talk to your body, and listen. Be a good friend to your body. Your back pain may be sending you a strong message: *"Back off!"* Your excess weight may be saying, "Lighten up—your life has become much too heavy!" Write a conversation with any part of your body you don't like or are unsatisfied with. Just begin, "Hello, the (tension) in my (head, back, throat, etc.)." Once these messages come through on a conscious level, you can deal with and act on them more effectively.

Hello, Body—Talk to Me!

Jan: Hello, Body—talk to me.

Body: Great. Let's look quickly at what's going on. Your circu-lation is out because you're not out circulating. You're a little overweight because you've allowed yourself to get bogged down. The stress in your back is from carrying too great a load on your back. Now, will you please just make a plan for handling these things and follow through with it?

Jan: Easier said than done.

Body: Oh, should I make it easier for you to do it than to keep putting my welfare off, then?

Jan: No, no. I'm listening. I get the point.

Body: And, by the way, I want you to stop asking me to hold back what you wanted to say but were afraid to. Storing your angry energy is really unhealthy for us both. Where do you want me to put it—in the back, or in the stomach, or shall we make it into eyestrain or blood vessel constriction, or what?

Jan: You mean it'll all catch up, sooner or later, so I can't afford to leave my feelings unresolved. Thanks for the reminder.

Feedback: I *am* my body. My new policy is: Say what I want to say now, and apologize later. Don't store it!

Another journaler shared with me a conversation she had with her body. "I've been operating under the assumption that my brain runs my body, and my body is just along for the ride. I have only been giving it attention when it breaks down or something goes wrong. My body told me, 'I need help! The only time you take care of me is when it becomes an emergency. Where do you think all that tension you put into me is going? Please, take care of me. Above all, ask me what I want—and then listen. I am your support system. We must cooperate.'"

A participant in one of my classes could not imagine how her writing could have any effect on her diabetes—until she wrote this piece.

The Old Body

The old body is acting up again. The sugar levels are consistently 100 points too high. I am out of control. How can it be that I measure the level, sleep seven hours, take it again, and it's gone *up* 2 points more! This makes no sense. There is something besides my food that is having a huge effect on my body's endocrine system. How can I find out what it is? My doctor cannot understand. But inside me is the key to it all.

Marian: Hello, you dumb body.

Body: Well, that's a fine hello!

Marian: Don't get huffy. Just get *real*. Help me find out why your stupid pancreas doesn't work.

Body: Keep calling me dumb and stupid, and I'll clam up completely.

Marian: Don't get cute—Wait, I'm sorry. I didn't mean that. I really do need your help.

Body: Well, what kind of help do you want?

Marian: The blood sugar level used to get real low so quickly with exercise. Now, I walk forty minutes and it stays the same.

Body: Tell me what you think about when you walk.

Marian: I'm bored stiff. Mostly work, I guess. Lately I've been making up all these snotty things to say to my boss. He pisses me off sometimes. And it does no good to tell myself he's pissing everyone else off too. I'm still angry.

Body: There's your first clue.

Marian: Yeah? What?

Body: You need to walk where the surroundings get you off this anger kick. Go to the beach. Watch the gulls. Feel the sand crunch between your toes. Then get the Accu-check out.

Marian: Think it will make a difference?

Body: Guaranteed. Now, let's get serious about the food.

Marian: Oh, nuts.

Body: No, you mean oh, sugar! You've been eating *all* the wrong things.

Marian: Stress = food. You know that.

Body: So what are you going to do about it?

Marian: I don't know, but I sure do have to take action. NOW.

Body: Get off the dime. Your grace period is just about up. You're in charge here. You know how to win. There's one more thing you can do.

Marian: What?

Body: You've been thinking about visualizing. Do you dare try it?

Marian: I'll do it . . . Oh, by the way . . .

Body: What?

Marian: I re-upped at the Diet Center today.

Feedback: My action is my feedback!

CONVERSING WITH ANOTHER PERSON

Another important and enlightening form of dialogue and communication with oneself is creating a conversation with another person. These dialogues can lead to resolving an inner conflict or sense of unease over a recent or longstanding difficulty. They can help you get a better grasp of your own position while gaining insights into someone else's point of view. Conversations can be especially useful when you need advice or guidance from an expert or mentor, and when you need someone to serve as a model for the type of achievement or success to which you aspire. They can aid you in appreciating the value of a past or present relationship. A conversation can also help prepare you for an upcoming encounter in which you want to be your best.

The following conversation was sparked when a journaler learned of an attempted suicide by an old high school friend. By creating a written conversation with her friend, the journaler was able to sort out her feelings of confusion and helplessness, as well as to express her feelings of support and friendship.

It's Been So Long

Tracy: Dear Lucinda, it's been so long since we have talked. I'm glad you came into my mind again. You meant so much to me when we were in high school. I doubt you know how thankful I am that you were my friend.

Lucinda: Imagine hearing from you after all these years! I suppose you must have heard about me on the news?

Tracy: Yes, and I felt so bad about it. I wondered if you could use an old friend out of the past to talk to.

Lucinda: You know, Tracy, I've always felt like I didn't belong. I should have been born in a time when I could have been a Southern belle—loved and cherished and taken care of. This alienated society we live in today is so foreign to my nature. Some days, I just don't know if it's worth it to keep going on . . .

Tracy: That must be a terribly lonely, desperate feeling. I wish we'd known how to really communicate what we needed when we were young. We could have shared our feelings of not quite belonging. Probably we would both have felt less estranged. Do you know, I never told you this, but it was your questioning and querying everyone's views and motives that led me to get my degree in psychology! I've always thanked you for that. Now, tell me, what is going on to make you so depressed? Can you talk about it with me? How can I help? You know, Lucinda, I'd do anything for you.

Lucinda: Gee, thanks, Tracy. You always were a dear friend. It means a lot to know you care. Life hasn't been easy since Roy passed away. I guess I have needed a shoulder to cry on.

Tracy: I'll always be here for you, Lucinda. Your friendship means so much to me, too. I want you to feel free to say anything you feel like saying to me. I want to comfort you through this troubled time. I love you.

Feedback: I didn't realize I needed to say these things to Lucinda. If I can find out how to call her, I think I'll try to get together and maybe say some of this to her in person.

Tracy's circumstances might have been such that it was inappropriate or impossible to speak to Lucinda in person, but that fact would not have lessened Tracy's need to express her feelings—for herself. The conversation gives her that forum. If she should follow through later and meet with Lucinda, she will have prepared herself to face a painful situation with courage and clarity. In another instance, a journaler may choose to follow up a private written conversation by sending an actual letter to express appreciation and understanding, or to share her experience.

Conversation writing works just as well with current relationships, whether or not the person you want to communicate with is able to communicate with you. The mother or grandmother of a newborn baby can write a beautiful keepsake conversation between herself and the child, expressing her love and her dreams for the child, and asking what the baby "wants" to say. The teenager whose parents don't understand him can write a conversation in which he shares his views and feelings, and imagines his parents' response. The goal in this kind of written conversation might simply be to open up channels for communication and respect, and to identify points of agreement and disagreement.

Communicating on paper can help to circumvent flaring tempers and unrelenting competition for the verbal "edge." Writing a conversation with a spouse or family member will enable you to release pent-up feelings, and get clear on what you are really feeling and want to say.

I Thought I Was a Good Mother

Me: Mother, I find it hard to be with you, because there's still so much unfinished business hanging heavy in the air between us.

Mother: Why, whatever do you mean?

Me: Well, all the feelings I still have about all the things I did out of blind obedience and a sense of guilt. Mostly it was guilt—that's why I acted so blindly.

Mother: Well, I don't know where you get that.

Me: I never felt I had a right to say no to you, or to suggest anything. Fear—that's all I had.

Mother: Well, that's how they did it in those days.

Me: Not everyone. You and some others, yes; but not everyone.

Mother: I thought I was a good mother.

Me: You were. You were fair, or tried to be in most instances.

The words I attributed to Mother in this dialogue are those she must have used hundreds of times. As I wrote, I could clearly hear her saying, "I thought I was a good mother." Right there, I began to reflect on "the good mother" and realized she never did anything purposefully to hurt me—nothing out of spite or selfishness.

So I came to know that, although Mother was not fine-tuned to me and could not empathize with me when I most needed it, she tried *her* best to be a good mother.

The growth came when I learned to accept her with all her shortcomings. (I guess she had been accepting me with all *mine* for years!)

I've been in many sensitivity groups, individual therapy and group therapy, but none caused me to focus on the situation through the other person's eyes. It has allowed me to know I was not being victimized, personally. When there's no victimizing, there's no need for anger. It's the anger that's crippling. I now walk on strong legs.

The main beneficiary is *you* when you write a dialogue like the preceding one. This journaler has obtained great value from her writing—whether or not she ever communicates her insights in person to her mother. *Even if her mother were no longer living,* writing the dialogue would be *no less valuable* to the writer.

For consultation on overall life direction, asking your inner guide or teacher is an uncannily effective dialoguing device. Instead of getting out the encyclopedia, reading another book, or seeking out someone else to advise you, look first to yourself as the authority on your life.

Choose a teacher or mentor to match the issue you are dealing with. When I was young, I used to idolize the comic strip heroine Brenda Starr, who represented for me the epitome of high fashion and glamour. Now I wouldn't dialogue with Brenda Starr about how to save the rain forests. I might choose her when I am looking for advice on the appropriate outfit to wear. You might ask Mae West, or George Burns or Red Skelton how to bring more fun and laughter into your life. Kermit the Frog could be your consultant on becoming more childlike. You might seek common sense advice from contemporary cartoon strip figures like Cathy, Charlie Brown, or Garfield. Perhaps you have a master teacher or mentor of your own to call upon. You may want to go directly to God or your Higher Power for an answer.

If you admire Winston Churchill's skill in diplomacy, Mark Twain's clever humor, Merlin the Magician's ability to materialize the invisible, or Martin Luther King, Jr.'s vision and leadership, you may want to invite that person into a fantasy conversation. Other figures to converse with can be a successful businessperson, artist, or celebrity who has been a source of inspiration to you. You don't have to know a Walt Disney personally, to let him speak to you as a visionary. When you write a conversation, you are really drawing from what you already know inside. You are just looking at what you know from a new and creative perspective.

Albert Einstein is an authority figure I often consult for his singular wisdom and genius.

We Are All Born Knowing

Joyce: Hello. I am a great admirer of yours. Even though I don't know much about you, I can see that you are very unique and definitely your own person. The reason I've brought you here to talk with me is that I need some expert advice. What must I do to move more quickly to reach my greatest potential for success? I want to make an important difference in the world, like you did.

Einstein: Well, as you might guess, I was *born* knowing. *We are all born knowing!* So what is it I have to share with you?

Read about me, if you like. I really want to encourage you, Joyce, to expand who you are. Throw off your self-imposed limits and start living more outrageously. Concentrate on being free of limits, and use your own fine mind. Keep your large vision in sight, and feed it by developing your dreams. And remember your favorite quote of mine about imagination being more important than knowledge.

Feedback: The dreamer in Einstein invites the dreamer in me to dream global dreams of harmony.

Another journaler chose Margaret Thatcher as the mentor who could advise her about her destiny. She received some down-to-earth suggestions:

Just Do Something

MT: Vicki, you know what you're here to do, don't you?

V: Are you kidding? I haven't a clue!

MT: It's quite simple, actually. I think you'll discover more of yourself by helping others get to know themselves better.

V: Oh? That sounds easy—if you want me to go to school for a hundred years to become a licensed therapist.

MT: Always looking for a way out, aren't you? Who said anything about being a licensed therapist with 100 years of training? I am talking about getting people to know themselves through their subconscious minds.

V: Well, that sounds good, but exactly what do you mean? By what method?

MT: You could make tapes with messages on how to open the subconscious mind, through hypnosis or maybe through writing.

V: Yes, I am fully aware of those methods and there are already people in those fields expanding them quickly. I don't know where I'd fit in.

MT: Oh, rubbish! Stop making excuses for yourself, and turn that mind of yours on! You know how to read and write. Use what you know. Take classes in one of those areas. Begin experimenting—on your husband, dog, cats, whatever! Just stop this nonsense of not doing anything because you "have to wait until you can be sure it's right." Remember, every action has a reaction, so if you're not acting, no reaction will take place.

V: Well, that's all well and good and most of it true. But "not doing anything" is still an action, per se, and my reaction is . . . now that I think about it, equal to my action. Boy, I hate it when you're right!

MT: Let's get back to the point. Helping others will probably be your "diamond in the rough" talent. But to discover it, you'll have to get outside the consciousness you're now in. Take some fun classes; get involved. And don't be so hard on yourself. Just be patient and trust your own instincts. After all, it's your life, and nobody else can live it for you. One soul per physical body—those are the rules.

V: Perhaps you're right. I'll take it under serious consideration.

CONVERSING WITH AN IDEA

Another kind of conversation that can produce very powerful results is writing a dialogue with any idea or concept that is currently affecting your life. For example, you might launch into an argument with your guilt. One client was able to help heal sixteen years of pain and torment over an abortion by writing a conversation between shame and guilt.

Another journaler used a three-way conversation with "Want, Need, and Desire" to clarify what she most wanted.

Desire = Want Fueled by Passion

Want: I want it all, I can tell you that right now. Yet I know I am lazy and unfocused, and that keeps me from having what I want. Sometimes I just have this general feeling of *want,* and I don't even know specifically what it is that I want. One thing I do know is that I want more laughter and play in my relationship, and I will have it. I want . . .

Need: Wait a minute. I think *I* should start. I represent the bottom-line stuff, like food and water, etc. I need healthful foods, warm shelter. I need hugs, nurturing, physical contact. I need stimulation and challenge and confrontation. I need to keep growing in a way that produces tangible results.

Desire: OK, my turn. I'm easy. I'm the pipe dreams, the stuff that makes life outrageous and full of joy. My job is to show you why you're disgruntled. I can be small or large, costly or free like a beautiful sunset. But beware if you say you want me and aren't willing to do what it takes to have me. I will start a war within you. So be conscious of me. I can bring intense pain as easily as intense joy. Once I am released, I am unstoppable. I can bring you to life, or I can kill you, or at least your spirit. Stay aware of me.

Need: I am the most basic to survival. With a little focus, I am completely attainable. Just be sure you put *me first,* or you'll be sorry.

Want: I represent the things in life that add flavor and spice. I can't hurt you too much if you don't have me. Often I just dissolve into space to become a new want someday. But if you let me become a desire, man, I've got you. I use passion as my fuel then, and it powers me like a rocket. Hey, Desire, does Monica have any of you?

Desire: Yes, she does, but she's been trying to sit on us both with that big, heavy butt of hers. She even tried cutting all the emotional lines to make sure we couldn't get to her. But we are still here, agitating her to death. If she'd just get up and get lively, we could move her so fast to a life of joy and fulfillment. So what is it going to be, Monica? Right now you are definitely getting your needs met, and you've got lots of wants begging to become desires.

Monica: What does it take to become a desire?

Desire: Passion.

Monica: Where's my passion? Why do I keep losing it?

Desire: You were born full of passion. Everything you did was passionate. But passion is threatening to those who have lost it, so they try to harness it. You are just starting to get yours back. The best way to kill passion is to side-track it. When it is out of focus or derailed, it just spins in circles, never burning out yet never creating dreams, either. Passion has to be directed to produce the results you want. Set passion loose in the right direction, and it will lead you to fulfill your needs, wants, and desires!

How about having a talk with Procrastination, or staging a drama with a cast of characters made up of all the elements in a dream you had? Dialogue subjects that can bring great results are joy, creativity, romance, success or anything missing from your life. You may also ask what you need to do to resolve a conflict or disturbance within yourself. Try writing a conversation with that song that keeps playing over and over in your mind, inviting out whatever learning or reminder there is for you.

One journaler whose efforts lacked consistency chose to dialogue with "Action."

Be God in Action

Renee: Action, what are you doing? What do you do? Obviously, you are the means for accomplishing a stated goal. What else are you? What don't I understand about you?

Action: I am so glad you finally asked! I have been included in your life so haphazardly, it is plain to me that you don't understand my full power. If you would use me consistently, the abundance and success in your life would be record-breaking. I am so much more than mere activity. I am *focused emotion,* in my purest form. I am such a powerful force that most folks drug me. I am what creates Olympic champions, life winners. I keep eagles in the air.

Renee: How do I access you?

Action: I am always there, waiting to be released. Simply stop drugging your emotions, and you will find me bursting at the seams to get out. You know, when people use the words "God in action," they are referring to the energy at the source of your being. Allow your emotions to flow, and you will reshape your world instantly. You will have endless energy, for your work will be your play. You have the ability to *be* God in action.

Dialoguing with an idea that comes into your mind, whether playful or serious, can be surprisingly beneficial. One day I was feeling harried, and I thought to myself, "There's just never enough time to get everything done." Now I have learned not to let a "helpless victim" statement like that remain unchallenged. I started writing a very serious conversation in my journal with "Time" to resolve my frustration. I ended up with a wiser, more creative and lighthearted perspective.

Time Is the Greatest Treasurer

Joyce: Hello, Father Time. How are you?

Time: I'm fine. Why did you see me as an old man?

Joyce: Must be because you've been around so long and you're so wise.

Time: I'm no wiser than you are. It's just an image that people attribute to me. If you like it, take it for yourself, too.

Joyce: Thanks. Great idea. Tell me, what have you learned over the ages about time?

Time: People view time very differently. Some use it as a weapon—This report had better be on my desk by 5:00;

I'm giving you to the count of five; If I reach the age of 35 without becoming a company executive, I'll see myself as a total failure. Some people capture other people's attention by figuring out clever ways to monopolize their time. For some, time "hangs heavy on their hands." Others use time to prepare. Perhaps it would help you to look at the positive use of time, versus the negative uses.

Joyce: That sounds like fun. Let's see . . . Positive uses would include laughing, learning, loving, hugs, sharing, watching children learn, cleaning and making things sparkle, planning classes that bring out the best in people. When I think of all these wonderful things, it occurs to me that time—and the way I use it—is the greatest treasure I have. During this lifetime I will use time to fulfill my destiny. Now is my big chance!

Time: I like what you're seeing about time.

Joyce: This is fun. Ragtime, showtime, playtime, time out. Time flies, watching the time. Time for my family, time to reorganize my closet, time to spend with each of the kids, time to thank everyone who has supported me. Time just for me. Personal time, quiet time, quality time—the gift of time.

Feedback: I like time. It's my friend—take a big chunk of it, enjoy it, use it, don't waste it, don't fight it. There's so much in life—I want more of it. Go on a TIME DIET—cut out the junk food and empty calories, and make wise time choices!

This preceding conversation is a perfect example of how we can take anything that seems to be working against us, turn it into a friend and learn from it.

CONVERSING TO DISCOVER THE JOY

Conversations provide a most effective means to writing yourself to a chosen result. Once again, start with the result. What do you want? What is the result you want to produce? Visualize it clearly. Put it into words. Then identify someone or something to dialogue with.

In writing a conversation, you can be less cautious and guarded than when you speak to someone in person. You can be carefree, fun and funny. You can try out words and new ideas without fear of failure or rejection. You can get out of your logical, step-by-step sequential way of thinking, and become more like a child spinning new possibilities from the threads of spontaneity and creative play.

What is joy, for you? When is the last time you can remember experiencing pure, undiluted joy? Your journal is a wonderful place to capture the joy you experience, and your writing will unfold in magical ways when you begin an imaginary conversation with "joy" itself.

Perpetual Joy

Joy, tell me what you are. I want to know you as a comfortable, familiar friend, to feel natural inviting you to share my life always. Joy—will you marry me?

Joy: I am not about talking, defining, reading, or writing, or anything else you might *do*. I am not about doing, but about *being*. Being fully, and allowing a full, sensual experience of a single moment in time.

Kate: Then how can I come to know you more intimately?

Joy: Pay attention, simply, to what *is*. Do you hear the soft sound of the water gently bubbling in the kettle?—speaking a warm welcome to all to help themselves. Smell that popcorn? If you should never get to smell that aroma again, would you remember it forever? Smell it as if it were your one and only chance to enjoy the pleasure. And the child sitting casually on your lap: soon she'll be grown and off on her own. Treasure each hug. Feel the wonder of it, the miracle of life that is yours for this moment.

Kate: I do know that joy. Sometimes I catch myself answering her endless questions absently, routinely. I can feel the difference when I kneel and draw her to me, and listen to her heart speak to mine. How could I let such an opportunity pass by without giving a thought to what I have shut out?

Joy: I am like that. I wait to be noticed and appreciated. When someone gives me attention, I glow and radiate and grow. And yes, I'd love to have you make a lasting commitment to me. I've been waiting for you.

Kate: OK, I get the idea. The shapes and shadows. The colors and the curves. The sounds and the aromas. The people and the events. The order of it all. The growth and the changes. To suck it all in, and cherish it.

Joy: No matter what exists besides me, turn and face me. Walk toward me. Embrace me, and no other.

Kate: I am rich with joy today. My sister, two months sober, reached out and touched me in a gesture that warmed old memories. The sun is playing hide-and-seek among gray clouds, and I call both beautiful. I can walk freely and free of restraint down the tree-lined street, shuffling among the scented autumn leaves. I gaze far and near, and everywhere I look the world is searching for peace. It is a time of the dawning of peace on earth. A time when judgment is transformed by love. I love what I once judged. The world loves where it once judged. We use our minds no longer to judge, but to en-*joy*. To recognize and share the joy of each moment. Oh, come on. Get real. The world is not all daisies and daffodils. There is plenty of crime and disaster and broken lives out there. You can't just pretend you don't see it!

Joy: Who knows more of true joy—Pollyana or Mother Teresa? There's a touching book called *City of Joy,* which grasps the deepest joy from the darkest depths of destitution in the tuberculosis and leprosy colonies of the Calcutta slums. Great tragedy and great joy. Think about it; would you rather be a tragic hero or a saint?

Kate: If it's just a question of focus, I'll focus on joy, thanks. Why don't I always focus on joy? Why wouldn't everyone?

Feedback: I can know joy only right where I am, in the present moment, and finding joy is always a *choice.*

There's no joy here, we sometimes think. How can I discover joy when I have all these problems, all these debts, all these things going wrong to take care of? Joy is not always apparent. You may have to search hard to discover it. You may have to give up resisting and fighting life, and just accept things the way they are, and find the joy in it.

Paint a New Picture

Me: Hello, Joy. I don't feel joyous right now. I've been building my hopes up over a possible committed relationship with Dan. I'm strongly attracted to him and fond of him, and tonight my expectations were disappointed. I feel down, foolish, and tired. What do you have to say to me, Joy?

Joy: Well, Holly, cheer up. This is not worth ending your day depressed about. You don't know the outcome of your life, so why bury yourself in sorrow when you have years of opportunities ahead of you?

Me: Yes, years of opportunities, ahead and behind me. I have grown and grown and grown. I'm glad for that, it's true. It's just that at this point in my life, I'm ready to share my future with a man, and I thought it would be the man I'm in love with. Now I realize I haven't a clue what he is thinking.

Joy: Holly, listen. Listen with your heart. When your head builds plans, has expectations, and gets disappointed, simply let go and listen quietly to your heart. Listen for the truth. Joy is always present. It waits in corners while your sorrow takes center stage. Learn from your pain, then go and ask joy to come out and play. Joy doesn't have to be loud or overpowering, so don't fear its intensity. It just waits to fill your heart with beauty. To help free you from the bondage of sorrow. Joy is your friend. It won't ask anything of you; it only gives to you softly. Joy is like music. It comes in many sounds. Use your music to heal your spirit, allowing joy to blend into your daily song. Joy builds on itself. Thus, when events bring you displeasure and disappointment, feel those feelings and balance your emotions by grabbing hold of the joy from one of the corners where it waits. All life is a mysterious process, and when you learn to trust the divine order of things, your grasp of joy will be firm and secure.

Me: I do understand that joy helps me break free of feeling like a victim of my circumstances, and I can change my sorrow and gloom by painting a new picture for myself, a lovelier one to live in.

Joy: Yes, you are getting there. You're still efforting, though. You worry too much. You wonder too much. You must *live* life—not by living in the past, even if the past holds moments of joy. You can remember them, but don't stagnate in them: it dilutes the magic. Capture life by living life. Do what you want to do. Keep your own counsel. If you want a lover who will give more time to you, then ask yourself what you've got to do to have that. What you've got to become. If it's still for you to be alone, then be happy alone. Holly, learn Holly. Let joy teach you the beauty of every moment. Even in sorrow, there is joy. How? In feeling the depth of each experience. Reach for joy. Cry in joy. Rejuvenate your spirit in joy. Give up the pain. You don't need or deserve to abuse yourself. So don't! Go for the great things you deserve. Don't settle for less, and don't blame anyone for not giving you something you need. Just keep going for it. Let go of pain, and try over again—and again, and again. Love thyself, joyously!

Too often, people think of joy as a vague future hope. Joy is a nice idea, but so elusive, far away and momentary. Like the bubbles that come out of the bubble maker, it pops the moment you catch it. So people fantasize "living happily ever after," instead of setting out to create joy as our reality and main purpose now. "Once I get a promotion, then I'll be happy," we think. "I'll be happy when the kids are older . . . when we find a new house or move to a better neighborhood . . . when summer vacation comes . . . after I reach retirement." A whole life can be wasted in waiting for the "right" time to be joyful.

There *is* an alternative: *expect* joy now. Although you can't hold onto joy, you can maintain the expectation that joy is always going to be there. That no matter what you're going through at the moment, you have but to look for the joy, invite it to come forth, and write it into your reality.

I Don't Accept This—Or Do I?

Playing with the Voyager Tarot cards last New Year's Eve, I drew a card I did not want. "I don't accept this," I said, and mixed the cards up to try again. And drew the same card! One more time, making three in a row! Coincidence??

Talking about those cards and that curious experience several months later, I took another look at the collaged picture on that fateful card: "Reflection." It shows an icy mountain, snowy pines, dark water, brittle stars, a comet, a barren planet on the horizon—a cold, arctic, icy, isolated scene. Yuck! I think. How distant and uninviting. Not desolate, but a sort of frigid, solitary beauty. The kind I wouldn't want to go to Antarctica just to see.

Its qualities are withdrawal, solitude, introspection, turning inward into self, rest, austerity, inaction, hibernation, tranquility, and peace of mind. I realize now that I can see that crisp, solitary vision right where I am. All those qualities compose a singularly fitting description of my life for the last year—like it or not. My response to being left for another woman after twenty years has been to withdraw, to mourn and to heal. So how do I bring any *joy* out of this?

Dialogue with Polar Bear

Me: Polar Bear, I know you go into hibernation every year when the winter winds grow too cold to "bear." You find a cave to crawl into and sleep. It is safe and snug, and you draw on the reserves you've worked to build up in your active seasons. But I always thought of your hibernation as a time of unconsciousness. How can such unconsciousness hold any joy?

PB: You *thought* more than you know. I have to sleep through long winter weeks to discover where great dreams incubate.

> While I rest, unknown even to myself, the new cubs are born and suckle and grow, to bound forth and play in the spring sunlight. Do you think just because there is no apparent surface motion that my heart stops beating?

Me: Well, I *can* say that I am becoming more centered in my solitude, more at peace in my "den," more at choice in my life. The wounds are healing and fading away, yet there are no new roly-poly dreams yet emerging. No bouncing play and no fantastic future aspirations. Still more *past* than future. More *present*—simple, unquestioned, just there—than either. That's pleasant, yet not miraculous or ecstatic. Not joy of great significance.

PB: Oh, you want not just joy or simple pleasure—but *significant* joy?

Me: Well, I suppose I do. Without significance, what is the purpose of it all? Significance has always had such significance in my life.

PB: Now, significance has never had much significance at all for me. So if you want my advice, go out and play in the sun before another winter sets in. Hibernating is not a thing to question. In the withdrawal you have been regrouping your forces and moving into your "home." But even a lazy polar bear doesn't sleep all summer long!

This writer has used her dialogue to move from "hibernation" into a state of readiness for action. She is opening to the joy, especially as she understands and feels more at peace with the difficult experience she has been through. Writing like this reminds us of the progress we have made on life's pathway.

CONVERSING TO ACHIEVE CLARITY

When indecision or living in limbo becomes too uncomfortable, when you're spinning your wheels and not getting anywhere, when you feel pulled in different directions by conflicting intentions, it's time to get clear on what you really want. So many people stay stuck in the frustration of letting other people or whatever event happens to come up determine what direction they will go in next. If you find yourself in such a predicament, you don't have to remain there.

One way to start is by choosing a destination. Decide where you're going, and make a mental map. Then draw a road map on paper. In bold ink, picture a major freeway flowing straight to your chosen destination. Picture all the side diversions and detours, with their different destinations, in a fainter color. As you focus on the outcome you intend to reach, this mental picture will help you eliminate the scatter. Do you want to wander down every side road you come to, or stay on the main road to your chosen destination?

FAME AND FORTUNE FREEWAY
Rehearse, practice, make right connections

```
     H          P          R          T
     o          a          e          o
     u          r          s          o
     s          t          c
     e          i          u          T
     w          e          i          i
     o          s          n          r
     r                     g          e
     k          Fun                   d
              but          T
   Dead                    o          t
   End        not          m          o
           productive
                        Harmful       R
                        to both       e
                         of us        h
                                      e
                                      a
                                      r
                                      s
                                      e
```

"She had a lot of
great excuses."

Another way to achieve clarity is to have a heart-to-heart talk with yourself, or the "selves" inside of you.

ME or me?

I feel myself slipping back into martyrdom again—feeling put upon, stifled, angry, resentful, powerless, defeated. It's bad enough that I'm feeling that way—worse that I'm acting it out, behaving like a jerk. I can barely cry. Poor me! I thought I gave up that behavior long ago. Well, a couple of years ago, anyway. (Actually, I've given it up several times!)

ME: Why are you resorting to this behavior again? I thought you were beyond that now!

me: Something jarred my serenity, and all my sirens went off, reactivated again.

ME: And what triggered that?

me: It's connected with the last time we went to Seattle and you decided you really wanted more time together with Phil.

ME: That was such a wonderful week. I felt we were so close. I realized for the first time that I want a living situation where we both come back to the same house most nights instead of his spending the majority of his time in Washington and me working in Montana.

me: And remember his reaction to that?

ME: Yeah, he said he doesn't want to "build a life in Seattle."

me: That's right. I finally let all my defenses down and really, for the first time in our relationship, allowed that I loved and trusted him enough that our commitment could be total.

ME: Wasn't our commitment total before?

me: Never. I always saw to it that there were spaces, distances, reasons for not being together a lot of the time.

ME: I thought those distances were just a natural outcome of job choices and work situations.

me: Not so. If I hadn't needed the safety of the distance, we would have chosen someone to be with who was accessible.

ME: I still don't quite understand what happened to you in Seattle, then.

me: Well, I finally came right out and said what I want, and got rebuffed. A part-time, long-distance relationship was all he ever really wanted. It took me right back to being a little kid again, to the time I found out it wasn't OK to let people know what I really wanted. I should pretend I wanted what I was "supposed" to want—I wasn't so bad off, was I? I "should be grateful for what I had," not keep asking for something else . . .

ME: All year, you've been peaceful—until Seattle. Why did this come up again now, and hit you so hard?

me: I *was* peaceful, because you were voicing preferences getting clear about what you wanted, and knowing it was OK to get what you wanted. It's just in that one final area of intimacy, being told "*not* here, not yet"—it doesn't seem possible to have what I want. Maybe I should just be satisfied with what I have, and let it go at that.

ME: So we're back to taking what we can get instead of getting what we want?

me: Sure feels like that to me. It makes me sad, makes me angry, makes me crazy. I feel defeated.

ME: Whew! That helps me understand how you've been acting. What do you need to feel at ease once again?

me: I need for you to be clear about what you want for us. I'm not that helpless little kid anymore. Love me enough to go for what we want and know that we deserve to have it. Help me to believe in ME.

ME: Whether or not it comes in the form of a commitment from Phil, I do know you deserve to have a close, fulfilling relationship with someone who is available and who wants to commit to you. That's what I want, too. So please don't sell out and settle for anything less.

Feedback: My own needs have gotten so muddy because I fell back into my old pattern of taking whatever I could get and feeling grateful for crumbs. The elusive lure of hope for an unavailable relationship is deceptive and unreal. I'll hold out for what I really want and deserve. I can have it!

Upon reading this piece aloud in a journaling group the writer, in tears, professed to a profound realization and understanding. By hearing and embracing an old destructive pattern, she became very clear on what she wanted and deserved.

When you are frustrated and unclear, another approach is to dialogue with the state you want to achieve. By doing so you may find yourself suddenly propelled forward.

Power, Please Come Forward

I really want to operate in the world as effectively as I know I can. I want to understand personal power completely. It seems that just as I think I've almost gotten there, something comes along to show me I have not come as far as I thought. I observe myself feeling more powerful with some people and in some situations than others. My power base is still somewhat unsure and too easily eroded. So let's have a talk with Power.

Joyce: Hello, Power. Please come forward and share with me. I really want to come from my strengths, and I feel you are definitely an important part of me.

Power: What is it you want to know?

Joyce: I want to know how to release you, so you are a constant in my life. I feel more alive when you are coming through.

Power: I must be *allowed*. Look how I show myself in nature. The power of the crashing waves, the strength of a gusting wind, an earthquake causing the ground to tremble and shake. The force of an avalanche. I also show myself as the sunrise and sunset, filling the sky with vivid colors and change. Electrical power is another connection for you to look at. A light does not go on unless the switch is turned on and it is plugged in. Are you waiting to be plugged in to your power? Do you expect yourself to be connected to continuous power without turning on the switch?

Joyce: Gosh, I don't know. Now I feel overwhelmed with all the possible ways of looking at power.

Power: What do you want to know, specifically, Joyce?

Joyce: I want to be as powerful as I can possibly be.

Power: Why not start identifying where you are with power, moment to moment? Start asking yourself often, "Am I coming from my power right now?" Make a list of the times you feel powerful. Work at increasing your awareness of your power and what conditions affect it.

Feedback: Naturalness is the key to power. I *know* when I need to be the earthquake, the sunset. Whenever I am paying attention to my own rhythms and those of people around me, power comes naturally. Power is relinquished by trying to be something for somebody else, be somewhere where we don't fit, do something we don't do naturally well, love something we don't love (being unnatural). Power is reclaimed by being natural.

When I wrote this piece, I was feeling exasperated at how slowly I seemed to be advancing toward realizing my dream. What could be holding me back? I needed clarity. Writing this conversation did a great deal to move me more firmly into my personal power. I became aware of times when I was trying to be "nice" instead of honest and powerful. I began asking myself often, "What exactly do you want, Joyce?" I realized that rather than just assuming others know and want the same thing, communicating my ideas clearly is necessary to claiming personal power. I told the painter what color I preferred on the walls in our new house, rather than asking someone who knew nothing about me to recommend a color.

CONVERSING TO WORK THROUGH CONFLICT

Conflict puts a person in bondage. It ties people up emotionally, and restricts their energy, locking it into the dilemma of attack—defend—withdraw. In a dialogue, you can get in touch with what is causing a conflict. You can realize what it is that's bothering you about a relationship. What is at the root of the pain or discomfort? Perhaps someone is being dishonest, using you, letting you down. Perhaps you are being dishonest with yourself, or letting yourself down. A conversation can help you identify the feelings and the issues—on both sides.

A young woman repeatedly felt aggravated with her brother-in-law. He would ruin family functions by raising disagreements and spreading dissension. I suggested she write a conversation in which she said exactly what she secretly wished she could say to him. The conversation she wrote between the brother-in-law, her mother-in-law, her husband and herself brought out a new realization. Her discomfort arose not from the actions of her brother-in-law, but from her own need to control the situation. After that, instead of letting all her holidays continue to be ruined, she admitted her reluctance to act responsibly and creatively. She finally released herself from the situation altogether. Now she plans fun and creative holidays with her husband, which they both thoroughly enjoy.

Within all of us is an inherent desire for peace, and because of this we seek freedom from conflict and resolution of differences. In our own families we have the greatest stake in how things turn out, and therefore these conflicts are often the most intense and emotionally charged of all.

The following piece was written in response to a good deal of turmoil a journaler was feeling about having a talk with her mother. She dreaded the disapproval and censure she anticipated. By writing a conversation before making the phone call, she was able to understand what she really wanted to say, which was to ask for help and understanding.

I Need Your Support

Mom: Hi, honey.

Me: Hi, Mom.

Mom: What's the matter?

Me: Joe and I are going to be separated.

Mom: Oh, no.

Me: Mom, I've been so afraid to tell you.

Mom: Why is that? Did you think I would judge you?

Me: Well, I know how you feel about my marriage and Joe and the girls.

Mom: I love you all.

Me: Mom, please don't make me wrong. I need your support through this hard time in my life.

Feedback: I was totally supported when I told Mom the truth. She's so beautiful.

Even a small irritant can weigh heavily on your mind. The next writer worked through a familiar internal conflict arising out of a social encounter by writing a conversation. "I could have stewed about this little incident for days, avoided meeting the man's eyes every time I encountered him and continued to feel worse about myself for a long time." Instead she wrote the following conversation and turned a potentially damaging situation into a positive one.

I Felt Pretty Annoyed

Sue: Hi, Kyle. I'd like to talk to you.

Kyle: Sure, what do you want?

Sue: I felt pretty annoyed with you last night when you acted like you didn't see me. I'm not invisible, you know. I want to know why you didn't notice me.

Kyle: That's easy, kid. You still act invisible much of the time. You are kidding yourself about it. If you want people to notice you, you have to put out the kind of energy that says, "Hey! I'm here!" Go up and say "Hi, I'm Sue. I've been wanting to meet you."

Sue: Thanks, Kyle, for your honesty. I also wanted to tell you that you don't seem very open to someone like me. You seem arrogant and distant, hard to approach.

Kyle: What do you think it means if I am that way? It's my way of protecting myself, because I'm just as afraid as you are to be vulnerable. If I seem so confident, it's just a mask that helps me function in the world of show business . . . I wish I had your "heart."

Sue: Really? I never would have guessed! Thanks again for your honesty. I feel so much better now that we've talked.

Feedback: This understanding may have been somewhere inside me before, but it's surely clearer after writing about it. Instead of judging others by surface appearances, I can just be real, and the other person will be, too.

This is the kind of writing that can help you climb out of the whirlpool, and rise above the turmoil and mental distress. Once you have written a piece like this, a decision may instantly follow: I want to change my pattern—now. It's a good idea to make a note of this learning. Make a refrigerator card—write your new options and post them where they will remind you that you have transcended this conflict from now on.

CONVERSING TO RELEASE ANGER

Once you have identified that your distress is about *anger,* and the anger has been pinpointed, you can write a conversation directly with your anger or its cause. Doing this can move you out of agitation and trying to figure things out, forward into action.

The next writer was triggered by a strong angry reaction to a radio announcer advertising a weight loss program. She realized that her disproportionate reaction indicated an association with some unresolved issue within herself, so she set out to write about it.

Letting Go

    Egads, that commercial makes me furious! Losing weight is easy—just stop overeating! They have no understanding of what makes a person overeat. But why am I reacting so strongly to a stupid commercial? My anger must have some connection to my weight problem. Maybe my last twenty pounds is twenty pounds of anger.

Julia: Hi, extra 20. What are you about? Why won't you go away and leave me alone?

20:   I am what keeps you under control. I am here to keep you where you belong. I keep you safe. You think it's from others, but mainly it's from yourself. You are more afraid of you than of anyone else. Julia out of control—that could be dangerous.

J: You are all about feelings, then.

20:   You feel things very intensely. You are afraid of your own anger. You know it might alienate everyone around you. What if you felt overly sure of yourself? You might not take any s––– from anyone. Your fear is that no one would like you. If you let your anger out, you'd be all alone.

J: So do I want to get rid of you?

20:   Yes, I think you are finally ready to let me go. This is a letting go time for you. Letting go of me and letting go of all your fears and anger and pain. It's time to push that stored energy out of your body, back into the universe.

    Feedback: I notice when I write I don't feel empty. I don't feel a need to eat. Writing kills the pain by letting it out of me. It's the latest, greatest diet there is: Write Your Dead Weight Away! It is time to unleash all blocked emotions in my body and soul. I want everything that is *heavy* out of my life. I love myself, no matter what.

What further writing and action would you suggest, if you were this writer? Perhaps you would want to write more about your blocked anger, or list all the things that feel heavy, and another list or action plan to eliminate them. You might recommend more about what it will take to love yourself even with your anger. The following journal sample in the next section was a second piece written by this writer about her struggle with anger and pain. Notice how she extends the issues and ideas from the original piece, penetrating deeper, and really working with her feelings until she reaches a conclusion.

CONVERSING TO RELEASE PAIN AND SORROW

When you recognize the feelings of pain or sorrow coming up inside, you can begin to release them by writing about what you are feeling. For instance, ask your body to speak to you: Where do you feel the pain? What does it feel like? Before you get into a long story about what happened, fully explore your feelings on paper. Then briefly answer the questions "Who hurt you?" and "What expectation did you have that was violated?" Write a conversation with the cause of your pain or sorrow.

Pain Prevention

My head is killing me! I hurt. I'm angry. Pete just called to say he was going to ask to work this weekend. We had decided not to go out of town, just to play tourists here in Somerset. I have been really looking forward to it. Now he says he has to work. *Chooses* to work. I feel unimportant. I feel insignificant. I feel taken advantage of. I'm always here for him. Waiting, waiting—and he expects it. Jeff is important. Matt is important. Julia can wait.

Julia is a "Woman Who Loves Too Much." Julia feels guilty about feeling and expressing anger. Julia waits on Pete all the time. The other day he waited on me, for a change—and was furious. So here we are, with the usuaual pattern: me giving all my love away to Pete. Dependent on Pete. Waiting for Pete.

Pete feels he is doing his job. I understand that, and it feels like his job is more important than I am. How can I get clarity? What is the learning here? What do I want? I want to be important to him. I want to feel special. I hurt. I want the pain to go away. I feel awful right now. My head hurts. The pain, the pain.

Me: What are you about, Pain?

Pain: I'm here to make you pay attention.

Me: Attention to what?

Pain: Yourself, your needs.

Me: What do you mean?

Pain: You are always saying it's OK when it's not. Stuffing feelings. Stuffing anger. It's harmful to you. It makes you sick.

Me: I feel worse now, expressing it all, than I would have holding it in!

Pain: For the moment, yes. But it hurts so much now only because you have blocked all those channels for so long. No anger, no joy, no intense feelings of any kind. So blow the anger through, and then watch the joy follow soon. Open those passages. Clean out the clogged system. That's why you're cold. You're always afraid, always pulled in to protect the core. You are paralyzed with fear. Let the anger roll out. Don't hold back.

Me: Why is this happening this weekend? This was supposed to be a special weekend. Why on our anniversary?

Pain: Well, what are you learning?

Me: I'm learning to be angry. I am learning to let my feelings go. I must express my anger and feelings. I hate holding it in. What is the lesson here? To let go of anger and pain. To let go of Pete.

Pain: Take care of yourself. Love yourself. Pay attention to me sooner, when I first contact you with my slight nudges and suggestions. Listen to my messages.

Feedback: What is true for me in my relationship with Pete? I swallow lots of anger and s - - - ! I sit on it, *weighting* for him to nurture me. It's over-weighting. I need/WANT to nurture myself, with caring instead of food! Pain prevention.

Another journal writer began her conversation with a migraine headache by trying to picture what this pain looked like. She wrote that it "feels like a dark stain that remembers secrets that dare not be exposed to the light. A migraine traces paths of pain I never want to travel again. It is a prison of pain, solitary confinement. Helpless. No sound, no movement, no light."

As her dialogue unfolded, it began to expose the long suppressed secrets to the light. She realized at last it was time to confront the childhood trauma that had previously seemed too awful to acknowledge. Her migraine headaches represented the tremendous impacted energy throbbing for release, and begging for a breakthrough.

CONVERSING TO RELEASE TENSION AND STRESS

When we talk about tension and stress, we usually think of these words in a negative sense, as something we want to eliminate completely. But beneath our level of conscious awareness, we may be harboring an opposite belief: "If I didn't have some tension, I wouldn't be producing. If I didn't have stress, I would lie around and not accomplish anything."

How would you function in a total absence of tension and stress? We can't live without stimuli. As you release tension and stress, what are you going to replace them with? What will your focus be on? Can you choose a more effective and empowering motivator?

Give some attention to the end result and the way you want to live your life. Can you imagine Walt Disney complaining about his tension and stress to meet the deadlines for *Bambi*? My guess is that he was probably too busy and excited about doing his work.

What end result do you desire? You don't have to know how to produce it right now. Just begin by getting clear on your intention, and the means for achieving it will follow. Would you choose to replace tension with free-flowing creative productivity? Would you prefer free choice to compulsion? Would you want peaceful cooperation, relaxed creativity, a manageable schedule, rather than the stressful conditions you currently endure? Write a conversation between stress and freedom.

I once wrote a conversation with tension and stress that arrived at an unexpected bottom line: My burnout was coming from a mis-directed use of energy. *"You have to burn from within. Burn in*—not out." For me, that meant I had to come from my integrity, from my highest sense of self. Whenever I came from my highest sense of self, I never experienced tension or burnout. This conclusion made a tremendous impact on my life, from that moment on.

What is your tension and stress about? I suggest that you begin by writing down your feelings and what is provoking them. Then go into a conversation with the individuals, issues, or events involved.

Let Me Out!

I hate the tension and stress that I put up with every day at work. The minute I walk into that office, my blood pressure goes up twenty points.

Tension: Ha, ha! I've got you where I want you! You're all bot-tled up, in my little container. (Laughs wickedly)

I: I'm ready to blow the cork of this blasted little bottle!

Tension: But I am just the perfect size, to keep you where you want to be—no more, no less. Can't you see that? Do you want a bigger container of tension, or what?

I: You have no idea who I am and what I want! I am creative. I am intelligent. I am more ambitious than these close-minded little parameters ever allow! I've got to have a way to express myself. I'll die of suffi-cation, inside the damned little bottle.

Tension: Well, don't ask *me* for your solution. I'm having fun in here, myself.

I: I'll call in Sledgehammer Sam. He can help me crack this case. Hi, Sam. Can you break me out?

Sam: Sure, it's easy. One hard blow to the side of this jar, and—wham!—you're out of here.

I: No, wait! I don't want to smash the whole works. I want to keep this job, stay here, and deal with it the

	best I can—if possible. Is there anyone else there who can help me out?
Genie:	(Enters, floating on air) Abracadabra, you said the magic word. What is your wish?
I:	Thanks for asking. I don't mind the hard work I'm expected to do. I just wish *somebody, sometime* would show a little appreciation! I want some praise and compliments. And I want people to trust me enough that they don't feel they have to use force and pressure me to get the job done.
Genie:	Is that realistic, in this situation?
I:	I don't know. How could I find out? I can communicate more. I can say what I want. (Maybe I'd better make a list of what I want, and make sure I know!) I could write a list of compliments I'd like my boss to say to me. I could decide to be relaxed and peaceful, no matter how anyone else treats me. I could estimate what I can accomplish, tell my boss, and ask her which work has priority. If none of that works, then I may have to consider transferring to another position. Gosh, thanks for opening the bottle to let me out. I'm going to call on you more often.
Creativity:	Well, I've been listening in all this time, and I'm glad you finally let me out of the closet. I can see that you might have to put a lid on me some of the time, to get along in this job. But you can use me in many other ways to create what you want, within the parameters you are confined to.

After you write your conversation to release tension and stress, take some time to notice if any tension and stress remain in your body. Most of us have experienced that appropriate physical exercise is one of the best ways to work out the tension in our muscles and relieve stress. If you are finding it hard to exercise, try writing a conversation between stress and exercise.

CONVERSING TO DISPEL DEPRESSION

If you are depressed, step back and look at yourself now with an objective eye. Is your depression in any way life-threatening? If so, this is the time to reach out for professional help. Use the resources that are available in your community. Seek out a referral from a friend or community agency, or use the Yellow Pages in your phone directory. Have a medical and/or psychological evaluation, and obtain treatment as necessary.

The following journaling ideas are suggested ways for dealing with less severe depressions that might not require professional help. Begin by asking yourself what the depression is about. When, exactly, did it start? What else was going on at that time? What does it feel like? Where does it center in your body?

When we try to identify what depression feels like, we might identify it as inaction, inertia, hopelessness, cyclical negative thinking, sadness, dejection, chaos, disorder, apathy. One definition states that depression is "anger turned inward." Can you identify any anger related to your depression? What issue needs to be resolved in order to lift the depression? What action must be taken? Begin by writing answers to these questions.

What is the part of you that is still inside there, alive and kicking? What does it feel like? What does it want? Try writing a dialogue between your depression and the vital part of you. Include feedback about your choices and be creative in imagining new alternatives.

Hello, Depression—Come Out and Talk to Me

Mary: Depression, my old friend, I see you have returned . . . what do you want? I seem to welcome you with open arms?!?

D: Yes, I am your "old friend" and I am here again.

Mary: There seems to be some comfort here with you. It's like a homecoming. Had I thought I'd seen the last of you?

D: I imagine you are comfortable with me because we spent so much time together.

Mary: But I don't want to spend time with you. How do you play? What are your rules?

D: I am an oppressive friend who would suppress your soul.

Mary: That's not what I choose to have as friendship! How can I diffuse your power over me???

D: When I arrive, you welcome me as an old friend. You have always allowed me to take you to your dark shadow space. To rob you of your power.

Mary: I met you when my body was in a horrible state of dis-ease. I remember when I first met you. I had no control over my physical or emotional state at that time. You sneaked in on me . . .

D: It's because no one prepared you . . . certainly not doctor . . . look on the bright side . . . at least you were not visited by my brother, despair.

Mary: I want you out of my life. Will you show me how?

D: Only if you are willing to do the work to heal.

Mary: I HAVE TO!!! Please tell me.

D: Write to the doctor who defiled your body. You don't have to mail it, just tell him . . . Write to your family, the ones that have shared your trips with me . . . Write to your 38th year, the one where you met me . . . and write to the 39th year, the one which you gave to me.

Mary: Will I heal through this?

D: Look at the rewards. As long as you stay with me, a part of you is being suppressed. I'll be glad to leave when you become clear about your role as the one who has the power over your feelings. Become fascinated with the idea that pleasing yourself is more important than pleasing others.

Mary: That's a lot of change for me.

D: Yes.

Mary: I will dialogue with the power in me.

Feedback: I see that there is indeed work to do in this area. And I have to do it. I embrace this learning! I am on the road to healing! Yippee!

This journaler transformed her depression from an illusive experience outside of herself to a dark, shadowy figure lurking in the corners of her mind. By creating this metaphor she was able to work with a mental state that had haunted her for years and begin the process of self-healing.

Through the process of living your life, unlimited ideas for conversations will come to you. Get into the habit of jotting them down and taking them to your journal. Pay attention: trust and tap into your own inner wisdom, your own natural knowing. Tchaikovsky said, "Inspiration is a guest who only comes to those who invite her." Instead of muddling around in the heaviness of any situation, you can *dance* with your creative potential through journal dialoguing.

6

Living in the Question—
The Art of Self-Investigation

"How far are the stars? How did they get there? What are stars made of? What does a star smell like? How long do stars last?" This kind of questioning is life to a young child who constantly pursues new information. Curiosity bubbles over, as the child learns, integrates and goes out exploring some more.

The child becomes a teenager. She looks up at the night sky and wonders, "Is there a God? How did this universe come into being? Who am I, in the scheme of things?" And years later, the teenager, now adult, implores the night sky, "Will my children travel in the heavens someday? Will I become a star in my lifetime?"

Questioning is an activity that checks and renews our spirit. In order to come up with powerful solutions, we have to ask powerful questions. The questioning attitude presumes an attitude of openness—that we don't know it all and we're open to new dimensions of learning, experiences, and information. Questioning invites the creative process. It starts with not knowing and creates answers out of the void or nothingness.

Someone once complained to me, "My life is about questions. What should I do today? What should I wear today? What should I cook today? I'm sick of questions. Why can't things just be simple and certain?" Questions like these show that one is living in dialogue with one's life, not settled into humdrum boredom and not living with anyone else's answers.

Someone who has stopped asking and answering questions has probably stopped growing and being vital. Creation holds suspense, mystery and the unknown. It demands inquiry and contemplation. It celebrates the questions!

In journaling, writing down the questions your life gives you provides a means of inviting your inner answers to come forward. You can have an immediate experience of the questioning technique by simply closing your eyes for a few minutes and asking yourself: "What question do I need to answer for myself? What do I want to know? What information do I need to tap into? What would I most like to get out of this writing?" Write a question at the top of a blank page and then listen. Allow the thoughts to come through and then write.

As you reread your work, what does it say to you? What is the main message it contains? What *Feedback Statement* can you add to bring a sense of closure to your thoughts, or to point out the next step? Go over your work and for emphasis mark important points with a highlighter pen.

You can write a long time on the following list of simple questions:

Am I happy?

Do I love the people I associate with?

Do I love the work I'm doing?

Why am I sad, troubled, worried?

What do I want?

What do I have to do, to get what I want?

I counseled a woman who was struggling with her grown brothers and sisters: "No one has any interest in what I have to say. My feelings and my ideas make no difference to them at all. They don't want to hear it."

"Well, is that true in other areas of your life?" I asked this very powerful woman.

"Of course not!" she responded with surprise.

"Then what does that say to you?" The question brought her back into herself. The comparison between her home life and the rest of her life was in compelling contrast. With her family she was running on automatic, feeling helpless as if she were still a child, not thinking independently as she was accustomed to doing in her professional life.

The *art* of questioning is foreign to the way many people were brought up. They have been given answers, not questions, and their questions have been suppressed, not encouraged. It is so rare in homes and social groups for someone to ask us, "What do you really think? What do you know? What do you feel? Let's get together and share what we have learned."

People go to counselors who have been trained to ask in-depth questions to reach into our inner psyches where hidden feelings and motivations lie. But questioning is an art you can learn and practice. You can practice the art of questioning in your journal.

SEARCHING FOR LOVE: QUESTIONS FROM YOUR HEART

The thing I remember most about my grandfather was that when as a child I asked him a question, he would put aside his shovel, kneel down, look with interest into my eyes, and give his full attention to the matter. Anything I had to say was interesting to him. There was no unacceptable idea, no belief that wasn't open to discussion and questioning. And he answered me with sincerity and love. He would never say to me, "That's a silly question," or, "Go away now, I don't have time." He would often follow a question of mine with another question, and wait patiently as I discovered the answers for myself.

Even if you never had an indulgent adult caring for you as a child, in your journal, you can become the questioning grandpa for yourself. It may take some practice to know how to ask the questions that nurture acceptance and growth. Those questions come from a place of love. They offer to listen unconditionally with a deep level of trust that you do know your own answers.

Grandpa, What Can You Say to Make Me Feel Better?

"Grandpa, what can you say to make me feel better?"

Well, honey, what seems to be the trouble? What's getting you down?"

"I've got so much work to do. I could never get it all done. I have too much to think about. I'm overwhelmed. Is there any way out for me?"

"Honey, I remember when you were little, you used to whistle in the dark. Nothing could trouble you, while you were whistling."

"But these worries can't be whistled away."

"How about whistling while you work, then?"

Try asking yourself the questions you would like to be asked by a person who loves and respects you. Cherish yourself like a nurturing grandparent in your journal. And explore the questions of your life as you write to come up with the answers.

SEARCH FOR TRUTH: QUESTIONS THAT DON'T WANT TO BE ANSWERED

People sometimes don't want to ask questions they'd rather not know the answers to. If I ask myself, "Why do I keep bailing my grown children out of trouble?" I may be forced to realize something about myself: I need them to depend on me, so they won't check out of my life altogether. I'm afraid of being alone, and I will do almost anything to avoid it. Fear of reprisal can stop many from searching for the truth, and it can seem better not to know. Serious questioning might be put off for years. But as you practice the gentle art of objective self-investigation, with the sole intention of learning and knowing, not of judging and making yourself wrong, you may quickly come to conclude: why *not* know now? I have nothing to lose—and everything to gain.

Why Am I So Hard on Me?

Beat yourself up before someone else does. That's the one time you feel safe. When you are already down in the pain. What can anyone do to hurt you then? You're already down and out.

Maybe that explains the craziness. It's safe, or so you think. If you hit yourself first, no one else will hit you.

But wait. Why don't you light a fire in the fireplace, and put some soft music on? There *is* an alternative to self-abuse. Nurture yourself. Take care of yourself. That's true safety.

Feedback: It's time to go back to see my counselor.

In addiction recovery work, there is a saying that the addict won't change until he or she is "sick and tired of being sick and tired." At that point, the questioning process will begin. The person can then come to terms with whatever facts have been avoided, and begin to direct inner resources toward asking and answering the questions that lead to change and well-being.

What Is the Deal with My Eating?

What is the deal with my eating? I feel full and uncomfortable and fat. I don't feel fulfilled. I feel yucky—obese. Why would I do this to myself if I loved me? I don't know why.

Do I love me enough? If I were a person who loved someone, how would I love them? I would take them dancing to music they loved. I would feed them a large salad every day, and fruit, with some protein and whole grains. I would invite them to tell me what their desires are, and I would listen. I would draw out their dreams.

Feedback: Treat myself like a person I really love.

Why Do I Shop?

Why do I shop? Sometimes I enjoy it, truly enjoy it. Other times it's an escape. And most of the time I'm trying to buy a self-image which, of course, doesn't work. Sure, the nightshirt is pretty and all that, but what does it do for me?

I shop because I'm lonely. I'm bored. It's a time filler. It's a habit that kills the pain and fills the void.

I want to feel good about my body and myself. Shopping is not the answer. I will stop dealing with my boredom and pain by shopping, and work to heal them. I will fill the void with other things I love to do, and make sure my shopping is purely for the joy of it, from now on.

Why Am I Crazy Today?

I don't know where I'm going. So many thoughts rolling around in my head. So many obligations, concerns. What avenues should I follow?

No one else can tell me what I need to know. I can go to psy-

chics, have my chart done, take classes—and what I really need to
do is just take the information I already have, and write to arrive
at a bottom line statement.

I feel like the March Hare, running frantically here and there
obsessed with the idea that "I'm late, I'm late, for a very important date." What "dates" can be important enough to work myself up into such a state for? No! The date is now. I will lie flat on
the bedroom floor, where the sunbeams cascading through the
window will melt my frenzy away. Then I'll calmly write out an
organized plan that puts sanity first.

Feedback: I'm so glad I wrote. It has brought me back to sanity.

Some questions do not lead to answers or suggestions for resolu-
tions at first. They lead to more questions. If this is the case, it usually means that more writing and self-examination is needed before
arriving at some solution. Yet, this kind of exploring marks positive
movement—from vague uneasiness to the search for truth and
meaning.

What Can I Do to Have Intimacy?

What can I do to have intimacy? Get a divorce. I don't want
a divorce. I want back a relationship with passion. What happened
to our passion? God, please help me do my part to get the passion back.

What is passion? High energy, excitement, newness, aliveness. I feel newer than ever, and so is Ed. What is wrong? Is it over
for us?

The following journal writer has taken the next step in her journal from vague uneasiness to identifying her feelings and recognizing
what she has not put into words before. Identifying the sadness is the
first step she must take before she can ask further questions and move
toward resolution.

Where Am I with My Body?

My body. My body is uncomfortable. I am too heavy in my
clothes. I am covering up the pain of losing Steven. Running this

morning, I felt it was difficult to lift my feet. My body would not respond quickly. I feel slow and sluggish.

My life is slow and sluggish. I am covering up my sparkle and shine. My fat is like layers of crud covering up the facets of a diamond. The glitter is buried. I want to clean it up. I want to shine from within and sparkle in the light. The glow of the diamond is alive in me. I want to be free to sparkle and shine always.

The truth is that I am very sad.

The beginning journaler may feel at a loss for knowing how to ask the gentle questions that lead to self-understanding. Let me reassure you that *you really do* know what questions to ask yourself. However, if you'd like a bit more guidance, you can start by choosing from the list provided at the end of this chapter.

If you're willing to commit the time and effort to both ask and answer your own questions, as well as to be your own teacher, you will find yourself within the wisdom or knowingness that brings you back to yourself and to joy.

QUESTIONING FOR SELF-DISCOVERY

A traveler was walking down a country road when she met an old woman skipping lithely along in old, worn-out tennis shoes and a long, purple gown.

"Hello," said the old woman. "How are you?"

"Fine, thank you," said the traveler.

"What does that mean?" the old woman replied.

"I'm well, and content with my life right now," the traveler responded.

"And how do you know you are content and well?" the old woman went on, turning every answer into another question. Life works in the same way, offering us a continuum of questions. Your journal is a veritable hotbed for sprouting new ideas and discovering who you are. You can turn every piece of journal writing into ten new questions, and write new self-discovery pieces on each one. Questions have a way of multiplying into gardens of blossoming flowers.

When the answer to a question seems out of your grasp, you may want to turn to a Higher Power for help:

What Am I to Do, God?

> What is my work, God? What am I to do? I know that I was sent here, this lifetime, to fulfill a purpose.
>
> The TV program about dyslexia was so good to see. The speaker labeled dyslexia a talent. I do believe our world is turning around when we stop labeling people disabled and start finding the talent instead.
>
> As I sit here in the warm, beautiful sunshine, looking out at the mountains and thinking about all the learning in THE FOUNTAINHEAD, I know that my purpose is to make this a world where everyone gets to have fun living to their highest potential. My purpose is to bring joy to the world! And my work is to be done effortlessly and with joy. Seeing the very vastness of nature, I believe anything at all is possible.
>
> *Feedback:* If God created mountains, water in streams and lakes, tall and short trees, and, of course, me—and I am created in his image, then what am I waiting for?

A client once shared with me that she sometimes felt so lonely that she would go to the grocery store just to be asked, "Paper or plastic?" She would schedule a doctor's appointment for a five-minute visit with someone whose job was to take an interest in her. Acutely, she felt in her emptiness the need to reach out for this minimal human contact. When she took this issue of isolation to her journal in the form of a question, she discovered a very loving and clear response—a big step toward resolution.

What Do I Want?

> I want a friend. It doesn't seem like much to say or write that, but to one who has never had a true soul-mate friend, it means more than words can describe. I wish Eric could be my friend— the special kind of friend I want and need, but, bless his heart, he just can't.

I want a friend—a woman friend who will like me and love me for ME, not for what I stand for or because of who I married. A friend who is vitally interested in the things I'm vitally interested in. Someone I can bare my heart and soul to. One who understands, truly understands. One who will share her life with me and let me share mine with her, and who is not critical, but will be completely honest with me. One who will laugh and cry with me. One who will truly care about me.

And I don't want the relationship to be one-sided. I, too, want to be all these things to her in return. I'd also like for us to be able to learn from each other, to grow, to be open to new things and to other people. I would like to have a friend who is experienced in being a friend, for I am not sure I know how to be a *real* friend. Oh, I know all about the surface stuff, but I want to learn how to get *below* the surface. Yes, I want a friend!

Our life provides us with constant opportunities to discover more deeply who we are. Situations confront us daily with questions of values: do we choose to sell our soul for profit or personal gain? Can we maintain our values in an arena where others do not? Writing a piece like the next one will help you to clarify your values and define your position.

Is There Such a Thing as Pure Integrity?

The question I'm asking myself is, is there such a thing as pure integrity? I feel I do have an understanding of what integrity is, yet I've sold out so many times in my life. In this job, the issue of integrity is a big problem for me. I try to maintain my principles, but it's a struggle.

How would we protect a person's integrity, if we set up a system to be sure all people got to keep their integrity? We would have a new morality: each person living true to who they are naturally and honoring the integrity of each other person to do the same. Where would that begin? For myself, it can only begin with me. I must live in my own life by telling the truth with love, for the highest good of all. When I can do this, I will never be separate from my integrity.

Feedback: My integrity, more than anyone else's, is very important to me.

WHERE AM I IN MY LIFE RIGHT NOW?

Ira Progroff in AT A JOURNAL WORKSHOP suggests journaling on the question, "Where am I in my life right now?" I have found this question to be an extremely valuable one. This could be one of the most important and illuminating questions you can ever ask yourself. It positions you. It gets you into the here and now. The more you ask it, the more aware you become. The more aware you are, the more you can become the person you were meant to be.

If you find that, "Where I am is not where I want to be," don't give up. Try exploring and writing to where you want to be. Ask yourself, "Where am I in my life right now?" and begin journaling.

I Want to Be the Crest of a Wave

Where am I in my life right now? I am a tree. I'm dependable, predictable, and my family relies on me for nourishment, shelter, shade, stability, aesthetic beauty, recreation, and tranquility.

I don't want to be a tree anymore. I want to be the crest of a wave: curling in the ocean breezes, whirling, tossing, crashing on a sandy beach, retreating again to repeat my playful dance, but each dance different, vital, energetic, never done before . . .

I want to be appreciated not for what I can give, but for who I am.

"Where am I in my life right now?" elicits the kind of writing that mines out the gems and sifts out the ordinary stones from the extraordinary. Like panning for gold, it draws to our attention the precious elements that bring forth our truth and joy.

I Am in a Period of Transition

Where am I in my life right now? I am in a period of transition—risking, growing, changing. I close my eyes and see myself as a child, raking and playing in the leaves. My dad is helping us, and every so often he tells us, "Come on, now, you kids, get busy and get this place cleaned up." We laugh and play some more. Everything always gets done even though we are having a lot of fun.

The next image that comes to me is a memory of being out in nature. I notice a delicate flower just opening up. I walk a little farther and see another flower opening. I look up and see the blue sky, and think with a sense of certainty that life is forever. Things begin and end, and there's no sadness. It just is.

I am conscious of my body feeling alive and good. The extra weight is not necessary. It is time for me to lose it, and I will.

My reaction: Work and enjoyment can go together. All things change in perfect ways, and I'm in charge. I have never been more alive than I am at this moment.

Now That I Am Free

Where am I in my life right now? I am tempted to say, "in transition," but on second thought, that is not quite strong enough. I have gone beyond that. The Ferris wheel of a year ago has become a roller coaster ride today.

In the past year, there have been so many changes. I have moved to a beautiful home and decorated it in my own fashion. I have made incredible friends, lost weight, changed my wardrobe, engaged in several new business ventures—the list is almost endless. Probably the most dramatic change is finalizing my divorce after a marriage of thirty years, when I thought I could never adjust even to a separation. I held on to an impossible dream, trying to mend the shattered pieces. I dreaded the thought of life without him.

Now that I am free, I feel totally devoid of the emotion I clung to so desperately in the past. It is a freedom that gives me the opportunity to move forward on my own—and it feels great. The ocean outside my door is splashing on the side of the house, crying to me to jump in and wash away the tears and replace them with joy and sunshine. My home is the perfect place for an uplifting of my very soul, which cries out to God in gratitude for allowing me this wonderful feeling of freedom and exhilaration. The growth available to me in the coming year is as limitless as the sea and sky.

If you are panning for gold and you find a shiny, glittering nugget, you stop what you're doing, pick it up, and hold it up to the light. You turn it over and over in your hand, examining it and admiring it, and wondering how much it's worth. In journaling for the joy of the moment, each moment becomes such a nugget to examine and appreciate.

I'm Opening Up

Where am I in my life right now? I'm opening up. I open new presents every day. I dream about opening presents and getting exactly what I want. The gifts are silver and silk and fun. I am ready to have it all. I see how I enclose so many of my gifts in boxes, and don't let the gifts come out.

Sometimes I'm afraid to be who I am. I don't want to offend people. But my feelings are evident. I cannot wrap them up. I shine like silver when I'm happy. I am soft as silk when I care. I am opening up to being more of who I am every day. Take off the ribbons and jump out of the box.

I *am* the gift.

Feedback: I feel happy when I am being myself. I always want to shine!

If your gold nugget is flawed with dirt and rock, you don't throw it out and start looking for another. You begin polishing it and smoothing down the foreign material to get to the valuable treasure inside. The journaler discards unwanted elements onto paper, writing out the gunk to uncover the value within.

Get Counseling

I'm stuck. I'm lazy. I'm lonely. I'm frustrated, and I hate it. Where am I in my life right now? I am alone in a world where no one understands. It's Thanksgiving today and I am the turkey. First I am stuffed with thoughts and ideas, then it all bakes away inside as I am roasted with pain. The words are killers: *debt, bankruptcy, failure.* I am afraid to tell Dad. Afraid he will say, ''I told you so'' and offer well-meaning advice.

Where am I in my life right now? I am tired and confused and afraid to take responsibility for my life. I see myself alone, because my "best" advisors have jumped ship since the troubles began. I don't want to give up everything, and yet I'm afraid I may have to.

Feedback: Get counseling, Renee. Call Monday. You need some sympathetic support.

Stored emotion often lights the fuse to blow away the hard rock around our solid gold core. People have to store feelings when it's not safe to share them openly. To protect ourselves, we master "nice" or "considerate" skills. But the feelings may burst through when a piece begins to "write itself." "It just amazes me that all that is still there," a writer will often say when the feelings begin to emerge on paper.

"I'm surprised at the sadness I am feeling," one woman said in wonderment. "I thought I had accepted my children leaving home. Blessed them on their way, and felt happy for them. As I wrote, I found myself sobbing, 'My *babies* are gone! I will never get to hold them, cuddle them, snuggle with them.' I looked through the old baby books—the sweet memories that are all in the past—and realized I had never mourned *my* loss."

Real Feelings and Real Concerns

Where am I in my life right now? I am frustrated and angry. I have made a major commitment in my relationship with this employer, and I'm feeling cheated.

I am sick and tired of giving my power away . . . to anyone. X#@# all this X#@#! I am not a stupid idiot. I am a real person with real feelings and real concerns. I am a person who from this point on owns my power totally. I will not tolerate being talked down to any longer. No more of this s———.

What do I want? I want respect and love. It's time to love myself a lot. God, let me know who I am. What is my gift? Why am I here? It's not to be a doormat. I am a beautiful, alive woman. Act like it. Be it. Get up and say what I know.

I am like a baby who jumps up one day and just starts talking. I am ready to jump up and talk today. No more diapers for me.

Own my power. I am OK. I am going to think for myself from now on. It is time to love me. Heal myself so I can get out there.

There may be lots of tears. They are coming now. So what if I cry? Tears of sadness, tears of joy. Self-healing. I open up to the healing. Then I'll be ready to do my work.

Feedback: I'll do the work. I'll write it all out and share with my counselor and get the help I see I need. I am excited—my healing has begun.

Have you ever been at a point in your life when you felt it wasn't worth it to go on? If you asked where you were in your life right then, you might feel like saying, "I feel like I'm at the end."

Notice that the next journal writer asked, "What's happening now?" which allowed her to become the observer, and moved her out of being at the effect of the events of her life into a place of choice and potential resolution.

What's Happening Now?

For those of you who have not yet met my friend, depression, let me introduce you to him. Yes, it's him and he is oppressive. Yet he's evasive and hard to name. But he brings with him a heaviness in my body and an ache that seems to settle around my heart, a gray mist that encompasses my body and stills my soul. He strangles my enthusiasm for life, my vim, my very energy. At first I fight his return. "I choose love," say I, and fight crawling into bed under the covers where the world could be held at bay. But all too soon the fight goes out of me and I succumb. I've watched this process, unable to quell its momentum. I have lost a battle, but perhaps not the entire war.

I met depression soon after a complete hysterectomy was performed on my 38-year-old body by a young male doctor who knew nothing about life or women.

No one told me. No one talks of such things. The atrocities performed on the female body!! I lived the next five years in a tortured body. Suicidal, I went from doctor to doctor. All's well, they said—tests are fine—this is perfectly normal—you'll get over it.

I felt like a rubber band stretched to its breaking point . . . like running down the street, screaming out my rage for all to hear. A fire burned inside me, and once in a while I explode with a violence I didn't know was possible. There was no laughter. Paranoia reigned. My family suggested I go off for a rest—perhaps a quiet hospital in the country.

A new medical report sent me to a new doctor—a woman. A wonderful doctor. She saved my life. She looked at me—and she listened—she heard.

Why now this feeling? Now, because my husband is with me constantly, demanding my every moment, prodding into my every nook, wanting my complete attention. Like a young child he follows me around the house. I've taken to locking myself in the bathroom to escape his overpowering me. I escape to the office to work. He follows . . . "Mother me," he says, "Worry with me, be my crutch. Help me, I'm lost. Tell me what to do."

The depression comes after he challenges my soul to a battle to the death, scorns my beliefs, laughs at my spirit.

But don't think I don't notice. I see that as I sink lower you fly higher. At last, at last you feel needed. The hero can save the day—but don't you see the power you feel has been stolen from me?

Feedback: I fought as long as I could—as calmly—as unemotionally to retain what I had worked so hard to earn. Until I could fight no longer. In retreat emotions reign. Yet this depression will only be temporary while I think, while I ponder, while I regroup and make my decision . . . to stay and remain myself, to submit and merge once again, or to run and start anew. To dance as one and walk as two is not the way we started our life together, and change is not easy. *Now* is how we should live—I can handle the now.

If you have ever felt "at the end," stepping back to see your life through the objective eyes of an observer is a powerful tool for realizing the options you have available.

Revitalization occurs by developing the art of self-investigation. Ideally your life would always be an open file. Encourage your own curiosity and keep asking questions. Within every question also lies the answer. By listening to your answers, you begin to see your life as a tapestry, and only by looking for the missing pieces can you hope to achieve a work of art.

QUEST FOR QUESTIONS

Questions always bring up more questions. How long must this keep going on? Perhaps for the rest of your life. A shift does finally come when you have more answers than questions. The more you question, the more you know yourself. Here is a list of some excellent questions to journal on:

How do I get to the question I need to ask?

Why don't I have time to journal?

Who am I today? Who was I yesterday? What do I want to be tomorrow?

How do I feel?

What is my body telling me?

How do I give up resentment?

How can I let go of my anger?

What's the best way to give up fear?

How can I forgive myself or someone else?

How can I know I am free?

How do I know I am on the right track?

How do I get where I want to go?

What part of me do I want to express?

What do I want someone to know about me?

What is love?

How can I experience more love?

What does spirituality mean to me?

What is wrong here?

What do I need to communicate?

What do I want out of today?

What part of my life is working? What's not working?

What makes my heart sing?

What is my dream?

What is it going to take to love myself no matter what?

What can I do to give back to those who have given to me?

What can I do to make a difference in the world?

7

Letter Writing—
The Art of Connection

YOU OPEN your mailbox. Advertising, donation solicitations, "Current Occupant" mail, bills. And—wait! A personal letter! In a hand-addressed envelope, the handwriting of someone you cherish. You pick out this letter, tossing the rest of the stack aside, and sit down to relish the next few minutes. Special words written especially to you. You celebrate a sense of renewed togetherness. As you carefully open the envelope, your thoughts do a quick flashback over the last letter you wrote, the last news you heard, the last time you spent together. Each letter strengthens your ties to each other. You share *who you are.*

You start to read. Suddenly, you are there. Picked up and transported to another world. Immediate, real, visual, perceptual. "Yesterday I sat watching the way the water laps so softly and peacefully upon the shore. You would love it here, and I wish I could show you these beautiful palm-lined beaches."

How wonderful, you think, a view of tropical splendor fleeting across your mind's eye. You read on: "But you can't come now. We are so heavily guarded, they have spiked all the roads. No one can come or go. This island paradise is shrouded in fear. Lately I can't be sure whether I'm being kept in, or I'm keeping them out. Jerry's life has been threatened several times . . .

You are gripped by a new reality. You have joined the writer in her experience, so tense and so real. The TV news stories about the coup were impersonal before, and so far away. Now you are personally in touch. You forget the sink full of dirty dishes. You want to know more. You are involved. You imagine what it might be like to be a foreigner sequestered in the middle of a revolutionary coup. Your own reality has been suddenly and irrevocably altered. You survey your suitable surroundings with renewed gratitude. Your life goes on, but you are somehow different. Broadened and expanded into a wider, bigger view of the world.

You pick up your journal and fasten the letter in place in it. Then you write a few words, as you often do, to acknowledge the feelings raised by receiving this letter.

You might not think of letter writing as having a place in your journal. But the letters you write and receive are a vital part of your life. They communicate what was important to you in a particular time and place, and what you wanted to share.

"I never write letters—it's a family joke," someone will say. "Don't hold your breath waiting to hear from me. I can't ever seem to find the time . . . It's not just the *writing* I resist; it's sitting down and scanning all the recent events, getting everything in order in my mind—that I must do before I even begin to write! That's probably the main reason I put off writing."

Yet letters are sometimes the only means we have of keeping a relationship alive. As a friend of mine once wrote, "Friendship, like gardening, requires a high level of maintenance. Attention must be paid or people tend to drift away, lose interest, or start a new life when you're not looking." Your journal is a good place to list notes about what you want to communicate in future letters. When you have a list of events and ideas as they have occurred to you, you have the basic outline or content for a letter. And when you use your journal as a central clearing system for your written correspondence, it unifies many disparate aspects of your life into one central location. What fun it is, too, to have such a record available at your fingertips, whenever you want to remember and recall special moments from the past!

Wonderful letters nurture and connect us. They are an investment of the heart, paid off in value that accrues over time. How often do people put reading the Sunday paper into their schedules every week, but "can't find time" to write to the special people in their lives? When we use our time to write letters instead of automatically turning on the TV, we feel rejuvenated and our energy is restored.

Who are the people you want or need to communicate with? To

stimulate the dormant letter writer inside yourself, begin by making a list of these people. Give yourself permission to choose the letters you *really* want to write and the relationships you really want to invest greater energy in.

Letters I Want to Write

My college roommate—say hi and rekindle shared memories
Joe—an old friend I always intended to stay in touch with
My brother in Europe—include the newspaper article I cut out
My grandfather—just let him know I'm thinking about him
My cousin Richard—reminder of our glorious vacation together
Ann, who is someone I never got around to thanking
Rita—someone I've held a grudge against for years—clear it up
My mom—fill her in on the latest news
My daughter—find out how she's doing and say I miss her
My ex-husband—wrap up loose ends

When you think about people you would want to write to, remember to include yourself! By writing love letters to yourself and saving them in your journal to read again and again over the years, you can take responsibility for giving yourself the love you may have missed out on and deserve. "How do I love thee? Let me count the ways . . ."

Here's an example one journaler wrote to herself. She takes it out to read whenever she needs to be supported, nurtured, and reminded of her goals.

Dear Andrea,

Now I remember who you are—bottom line—I love you. Filling all your thoughts and mind with the love that starts right inside and has nothing to do with anyone else or any circumstance. Centering and aligning yourself with that love. Seeing beyond the external appearances into the "heart of the matter"—all is love, and thou art that.

The power of your word lies in your commitment to act:
   1) Communicate with your mother complete forgiveness, understanding, love, freedom.

2) Love yourself, care for, recognize, and encourage that precious part of you that is all loving, energetic, creative, vital, vulnerable, courageous, forgiving, one with all.

3) Reestablish all family relationships on a premise of unconditional love and support.

4) Now's the time to move from the space of knowing to the space of risking, doing, growing.

All the power is yours. Put yourself out there!

> I love you,
> Andrea

LETTERS TO SAVE

What are the letters you save? You don't have to be an accomplished writer to create a letter that someone will love to receive. Being able to write well is not the key to creating letters that touch someone's heart.

The following unedited letter was written by a seven-year-old to her aunt. What is it that makes children such natural letter writers? It has nothing to do with their schooling, or mastery of the written language. Children's letters demonstrate that it is the communication of our feelings that is most meaningful.

Dear Aunt Nancy,

How are you? I'm fine. What are you doing? I'm working hard at school, and having fun playing in the sun. How about you? Are you getting excited about the wedding? I sure am. The dresses are beautiful and we both love them. I was wondering what color should the shoes be?

> Love,
> Vanessa

What is it that we treasure about letters like this? They overflow with shared love. They connect us with the news in a personal way—

whatever the writer considers important. They *give* a gift from the heart. We are touched by their pure simplicity.

You might want to have a look at the collection of old letters you have saved. Is there a packet of treasured love letters in a trunk in your attic? Are letters stashed in the back of a dresser drawer? Stored in a shoebox? Dropped into various files? What qualities make these letters special to you? What can you learn from them about writing letters that someone might want to save?

LETTERS FOR SPECIAL OCCASIONS

Have you ever written a letter, drawn or painted a picture, or made your own Valentine in place of buying a commercially produced card? Your creations can be infinitely more personal, and are often more poignant, beautiful, and fun, too.

Even when you are living in the same house with someone, you may communicate differently in a letter than you would in person. Letters enrich both yourself and others. Letters summarize, capsulize, and concentrate our experience. Letters document relationships. Letters are great for hellos and good-byes. Letters can mark milestones—a special birthday, or graduation.

Dear Daniel,

How proud I am to honor your graduation today. I see you walking down the aisle with your head held high. Well have I known you with your head bowed low in pain and sorrow, yet you did not shadow your eyes with shame. I thank you for the privilege of sharing your sadness and joys. The fullness of feelings has been a rich part of our growing together.

I see you walking down the aisle placing one foot in front of the other so deliberately, with outward confidence and precision, though perhaps with some inner doubts and fears mingled in with the glory of your success. It reminds me of the very first baby steps you ever took, teetering on tiptoe off into the grass. You fell many a time, but nothing could discourage you from pulling back up to set off on your own two feet again. Through all our shared doubts and fears over the years, I have watched your strengths and skills develop, and I am thankful that in sharing your weaknesses, you have developed profound strengths. Strength to walk down the aisle of life continuing to place one foot in front of the other through whatever struggles and distractions may come your way, with your vision set on your own life's goals.

Yes, I am proud of you, my son. Proud of your gentleness, proud of your honesty and the depth of your understanding, proud of your willingness to let others win through knowing you, proud of the struggles you've mastered and the goals you've achieved. Most of all, proud of the pride you have learned to take in yourself.

I honor the milestone you have achieved today. Let us acknowledge that from this point on, you will walk down the aisles of life as an independent adult. You are no longer my baby boy. From now on, you will always be my beloved adult son. Free to be *you*. Know that I will always love you, and you will always have a special place in my heart.

Love,
Dad

In our society, we occasionally hold formal ceremonies to officially acknowledge rites of passage such as graduations, bar/bat mitzvahs, and other steps toward maturity. But all too often, our stages of growth pass almost unnoticed in any personal way among the people they affect the most. If we begin to write letters like the preceding one to mark our milestones of growth—the baptism of a child, first words spoken, first day of school, awards and honors, confirmation, memorable acts of generosity, first high heels or tuxedo, turning thirty, etc.— we can open up and express the full range of our feelings about them. This turns our growth into a conscious, rather than an unconscious, process. We imbue a sense of certainty and assurance into our own evolving personal identity.

Such letters beg to be saved. If you write such a letter to a child, ask the child to write one also. Then you can start a special journal for each child, and attach these letters in it to preserve them for a time when the child is grown. I have a friend who corresponds actively with many of her relatives and friends, and over the years she has compiled personal journals for each person, filled with wonderful memories. No one is ever bored visiting her.

Pressed into my husband's baby book is a letter from an uncle who wrote simply to say, "We're glad you're here." Letters can solidify the sweetness of beginnings and endings, instead of avoiding the discomfort of unfamiliarity and the pain of separation. How different we may feel if, instead of ignoring the major and minor comings and goings of friends and relatives, we write a brief note to send a thought from the heart and commemorate them.

Dear Jay,

   Tricking the trick-or-treaters, warding off old lady Gray's verbal assaults, rounding up escaped hamsters, late nights of pinochle and popcorn, rideshares to Cub Scouts—together we make a great team.

   I love you guys, and I'm going to miss you a lot. Memories of our good times together will always be a highlight of our days in Spokane. Life moves on, but I won't forget you. You have been a treasured part of my life these past years. I hope we will manage somehow to keep in touch.

Love and laughs,
Sam

LETTERS FOR RELEASE

One of the most valuable results of writing letters is to free up buried energy, allowing you to think and feel things through. This may not lead to immediate resolution or inner peace, but it will lead to change. In relationships, what is left unexpressed has a tendency to preoccupy us subconsciously. Simply expressing our thoughts and feelings, even without expectation of any response, can be very therapeutic and healing.

Dear Eve,

   I'm writing this letter because I have such a need to communicate with you. So much has happened in so little time. I want you to look closely at who you are and what you represent, until you can be reassured that what "happens to you" comes about through your choice and your direction.

Ever since last September you've been fighting the control you felt from Don. I can't even begin to tell you the pain I feel, seeing your body so racked by tears and anguish. All I know is that you are fighting for your own survival and identity.

Nor do I understand why growth may be so painful. I only know that the thing that brings me back to sanity is to sit down and write—until an answer surfaces. This is my advice to you, as to myself. *What is the gift?* Keep asking that question until it has been resolved.

Why have you chosen two men, so different and so alike, to be your teachers? I want you to write *for days,* if necessary, to find the answer. Just trust in God, turn it over, write, and then act for the good of all concerned.

In the meantime, I am here for you one hundred percent, if you want to turn to me for strength whenever yours wavers. Call me when you need help with the kids—anything at all. I love you very much.

> Love,
> Mom

After writing a letter like this, journalers commonly comment, "Wow, I hadn't realized until now that this writing was for *my* release! I'm amazed how much better I feel, having put my feelings and concerns into words. I didn't know I was so angry. Maybe I need to write more like this. I hope now I can offer support and not add my anger to the problem!"

THE UNSENT LETTER

When we have difficulty communicating our needs and wants, writing a letter we never intend to send is an excellent way to organize and clarify what we really want to say, without having to edit our thoughts to avoid hurting or offending someone. Here, too, writing may turn out to be more for ourselves than anyone else.

The next journaler wrote an unsent letter to create some changes she wanted to see in her marriage and prepare her for the next step.

Dear Doug,

The following is a list of things I want you to know regarding what I need in our relationship.

I need a lot of tenderness—especially in your kisses and the way you hold me. I need to feel more connected when we make love. It almost seems sometimes as if it's a chore for you, or you're embarrassed by it. I don't like feeling like I'm with a fifteen-year-old boy who makes "artillery" sounds and gropes my body. Sweet sensual whispers and soft caresses are what I long for. I truly crave the romantic side of you that I haven't seen in so long.

I need for you not to act so defensively when I ask a simple question. If you don't want to answer it—just say so.

I need to know what you need!! So we can really rely on each other.

I need you to support me in my career, and give me the freedom to do what I must do to be successful in it.

I love you very much, and I want you to know I would never do anything to hurt you. Let's talk more about what it is that we both need. I want to be happier, and I want you to be happier too.

Love,
Kelly

An unsent letter allows you to say whatever you feel like saying, uncensored, right out. Afterward, you can always revise your message for tact and sensitivity. You can decide *how* you want to communicate after you have specified *what* you want to communicate.

WISDOM LETTERS

Communication blocks with people we care deeply about can sometimes be circumvented in a thoughtfully worded letter. The next writer uses a kind of writing which might be called a "wisdom letter" —a letter that brings forth her own inner wisdom to unlock the feelings and love she has for her pre-teenage granddaughter. Her purpose is to express the depth of her caring and understanding, and start the flow of communication which had seemed to reach an impasse.

Dear Katy,

I am writing because I care about you so much, and I've been noticing lately that Grandpa and I and your mom can't seem to laugh and talk and feel good with you as much as we used to, because you seem to be angry so much of the time. It troubles me a lot to see you so unhappy, and I am hoping that my thoughts about it may help us to understand each other better.

I know you're only ten years old, but in so many ways you are much older than that. You have been through so much in those ten short years, it has made you grow up fast. And I know you are very intelligent, so I am going to write to you as if you were an adult. I think you can understand, if you want to. And I really hope you do, because I want so much for you to grow up and be a happy, satisfied person.

It may sound funny to you to hear this, but, Katy, when I was little I was a whole lot like you. I was always being disciplined for being so strong-willed. (I got spanked with wooden hangers, my mouth was washed out with soap a lot, and my mom threatened to send me to Juvenile Hall if I didn't start talking more nicely.) I realized much later that we never did talk to each other. She just told me how she expected me to act. She never listened to how *I* felt, and why I was acting the way I did. It would have meant so much to me to have someone to express my feelings to, someone who cared and wanted to listen, but I never did. I'm wondering if you feel the same way too, sometimes.

I have a strong feeling that you are angry because you'd like things to be different between your mom and dad. And that you want to fight it because they aren't. Fight it and blame your mom, and stay furious at her, as you hold on fiercely to your love for your dad. It seems like you resent everyone except your dad, for not giving you what you want. I know you feel your mother is not taking good enough care of you, that she doesn't give you enough time and attention and money. Yet the people you resent, especially your mom, are trying so hard to do the best they can, but you don't see this, because your eyes are filled with anger. I hope I can persuade you to look beyond your anger for a minute and think about another way of seeing things.

Katy, honey, your mom is having a hard time too—just like you. It's a big responsibility to be a single parent and take care of you and your sister alone, working so hard to make all the money it takes to support a family on top of that. When she married your dad and started a family, this wasn't how she planned for things to work out. It is a big adjustment for all of you. It hurts your mom, too, that she can't give you as much as she'd like to be able to right now. She, too, wants you to be happy. But the divorce happened, and even though it's a hard fact to accept, she is picking up the pieces and doing the best she can to build a new life with you and your sister.

And that's a choice I hope you will make someday, too. You see, honey, in all of life you can either accept the way things are (if they can't be changed) and find a way to be happy anyway, or fight them and be miserable. Each person makes this choice, and each person makes their life just the way they want it each time they make this choice.

The way you choose, each day, is so important, Katy. You can help your mom and your sister so much, by trying to be understanding and doing what you can to make things better. I suspect it would make you happier, too.

It's OK to feel angry sometimes, honey. I understand how disappointed you have been. But do you think it will help anyone if you stay angry a very long time? I hope you will come and talk to me about your angry feelings, so you can let them out and let them go.

Then I want you to talk to your dad. Tell him that you need him to give some money every month for your food and clothes. Most fathers want to be responsible for taking care of their children after a divorce. They don't just walk away from their children and forget what they need. They pay what is called child support payments.

I know I'm asking you to act like an adult, but I don't think it's fair for you to blame your mom who is doing all she can to support you, and not ask your dad for anything. If you don't want to do this, then I think it will be very necessary for you to do all you can to help your mom by making the most of the money she does have and helping to make your home a happy home.

I know you'll be so much happier when you feel good about yourself and start taking more responsibility for yourself and being helpful to others. Once you show that you can be counted on, that you really want to work and succeed, you'll be making a giant step toward growing up. People will trust you to babysit and do other jobs. You'll be able to earn your own money, and buy more of what you want—all by yourself! And I imagine you might be very surprised at how much more fun it is to be smiled at and hugged, than to be yelled at and restricted.

I love you, sweetheart. Please call or write to me, and let me share what you're thinking. Perhaps we can plan to do something together soon—just the two of us?

Love,
Grandma

We struggle sometimes to get beneath our anger and express our pain instead of moving our minds beyond thoughts that attack, justify our position, and make the other person seem wrong. We want to speak from a deeper, more objective understanding using words that will fall upon receptive ears. We want to bring healing and release to a relationship that has been disrupted by misunderstanding and anger.

The next writer struggled with this very problem, and her "wisdom letter" to her young adult stepson reveals the evolution of her struggle.

"My wish is that someday he will say, 'Oh, my God! Now I understand and appreciate you.' But even if he never does," she said after sending off the letter, "I feel a great relief from saying what I needed to say and had been holding back for so long." Writing the letter helped her to be focused and clear, to see the real issues that were facing her: the necessity of understanding and healing the lingering effects of alcoholism and codependency in her family relationships. The letter sets this healing in motion.

Dear Timothy,

It has been so long since I felt I could really communicate with you. There are some things I want to say to you, and this letter will be my best attempt. A pattern has developed when we have tried to sit down and talk with you that I find very disturbing: your dad agrees to give you anything you want, on some conditions that are forgotten as soon as you get it. Then later when we get aggravated again, we talk about what went wrong, and more empty promises are extracted.

This, of course, works to serve only one purpose: that your dad will never have to risk losing your "love." As long as he feels he must buy your loyalty at any price, he is acting out of fear of loss, not out of the responsibility of being a good parent. He cannot make decisions that are in either his or your best interests. The best he can do is pacify the situation and make himself feel better until the next big blowup. But in the long run, in this kind of self-deception, everyone loses, because what is bartered away is our integrity and ability to believe in ourselves.

This pattern is just a way of denying what really is, and avoiding taking the necessary actions to solve problems. It has meant that you could have everything your way, without consideration for anyone else, as long as you agreed to play along with his game and not threaten the way he had it set up.

This has been a battle I've struggled with for many years, without the slightest success. Me saying, no, you can't have the car (or whatever) because you haven't met what we agreed upon as the requirement for that privilege. And your dad stepping in and saying, "Oh, you poor baby, just go ahead and do this ten-minute job and you can still have what you want, anyway. Just promise you'll do better next time." That stinks! It says to you that you can do anything you want without responsibility to think about anyone else's needs.

I know it was my responsibility to say to you that since you didn't keep your end of an agreement, you would have to deal with the logical consequences. (If you didn't buy a gift to take to the Christmas party gift exchange, for example, you would have to suffer the embarrassment of arriving without one.) This is absolutely essential, I know for sure, for a person to learn to cope with the real world. And with your dad always intervening to make sure you could always get what you wanted in spite of everything (going out to buy a gift for you each year when you neglected to think of it!), this has put me in an untenable situation. I hated it. Dad got to be the good guy, "the one who really cares about you and wants you to have what you want," while I stood alone on my integrity in the role of the family bad guy, the wicked stepmother stereotype, reenacted once again with the same inevitable unhappy ending.

Tim, there is a very simple reason why your dad is unable to say no to you. You see, your dad is *addicted* to fantasy. I don't know how able you will be to understand the explanation for this. He *has* to believe everything—especially he himself—is wonderful and beautiful and loving and giving, "practically perfect in every way." That real life is a fairy tale. It's the addiction that makes him unavailable to deal with the intense anger he holds locked inside himself, as well as any unpleasantness from anyone else. So when he does things that hurt other people, he must remain oblivious to the effects of his actions, denying them completely. Or turn his attention away from troublesome matters, and start a new project that will be exciting and different, so he can leave behind the mess of a situation he's created and not have to think about it anymore. Buy a new toy, go somewhere different—if the rest of your life is screwed up, leave it behind to take care of itself.

So his addiction has him clinging desperately to the illusion that everything is fine—and needing other people to help him maintain it. It means that he is always—and always will be, until and unless he breaks through it by doing some painful work on himself—preoccupied with meeting his *own* addictive needs. He is available to other people only insofar as they enable him to meet those needs: they worship him and call him wonderful and go along with whatever *he* wants. God forbid that they should have needs of their own—there's no room in an addiction for other people's needs. Except, of course, for occasional trade-off arrangements.

I am sorry if you feel hurt and rejected, but there is no winning with addiction—only self-deception. I am sorry I have been unable to give you what you needed, but there was no winning for me in the game, either. I had to step out of it and figure things out. Once I understood all this, the game was up. I quit playing.

I always hoped that I could be a "real" mother to you kids. That all I did would be appreciated one day. I guess I still do, although I now realize that it was my own low self-esteem that allowed me to support the losing game for so long.

This is not an easy time in my life, I don't know how much you may realize. But it is a time for me to stop playing losing games. I want to have people around me who are eager to contribute and share in the work and responsibilities. I *need* to be around people who carry their own weight, and pay their own way. I am recovering from an unhealthy rescuing need myself. I want people who keep their word and do what they say they will do—the same as I do in my life. I am weary of bearing all the burdens myself, and then being criticized for not doing it well enough. It is time for me to stop supporting any compromises of my integrity, and stop taking on responsibilities that rightfully belong to you and others.

I would encourage you to go and get some counseling. Your dad and I were both raised in alcoholic families, meaning that the ways we learned to relate were filled with denial of reality and victim/rescuer/enabler types of interaction. It's something I've been working very hard to heal for a very long time. Sad to say, it's been the ways you've learned from us, and there is the same healing work for you to do, too. And you can only heal it by becoming aware, understanding what you're doing and thinking, and choosing to change things out of that new awareness. Many Adult Children of Alcoholics groups and books on this subject are available now to provide valuable help and support with the process.

It's important to get to work on your healing right away. It's by far the most important job you can do, and until you do it, your life will be limited by unexamined, old repeating patterns leading only to frustration and failure. Family Service Association has a sliding fee scale. Call them—and commit steadfastly to your healing.

I believe you do have potential in your life for achieving important things. You have a bright, intelligent mind and a good heart, and a wonderful congenial manner. But I am concerned about choices you have made in recent years which have undermined your own self-respect so badly. I hope most of all that you will come to see yourself as an adult person ready to give back to the world some of the goodness and talents you have received.

I apologize if this sounds preachy to you. The best I can do is to say what I need to say to you in the most thoughtful words I have been able to formulate. I have thought a great deal about this, and I hope you will, too. I'd love it if you would take the time to write back to me.

The truth is, I have felt hurt and alienated from you more and more, as you have chosen in your life things that seem so far from what I value and consider important. Yet my wish for you is not to come out of my mold, but that you discover how to live in a way that you have respect for yourself and live up to your own potential.

It is up to you, and you alone. I wish you success.

Love,
Sarah

In a wisdom letter like this, we can answer the questions, "What is it that disturbs me so? What are my true feelings? What are my options?"

The writer was glad she had written the previous letter because, when her teenage niece confided that she felt lonely and misunderstood, she knew that the insights she had developed might be valuable to her niece, too. She was excited at the opportunity to share what she had learned. She wrote:

Dear Bonita,

Your mom doesn't understand you, you say. She doesn't listen to you, and she doesn't hear what you want to say. What you wrote reminded me of myself when I was a teenager. I felt so lost and angry, but all I knew how to do was just hang around, hoping my mom would notice me and show some interest in what I was thinking.

Yet I know in *her* mind, she thought she was doing everything to be a good parent. She always provided good meals and clothes and lessons, and she came to all our recitals and school performances.

Now I realize: she really didn't have much idea of what is important to an older child or teenager. In her generation, no one talked much about how they felt. My hanging around probably just made her uncomfortably aware that she didn't know what to say to me, how to really communicate.

Your mom grew up in the same way, honey. No one talked to her, I mean in a personal, caring way. But in her family there was another disturbing thing: her father drank too much. I mean, got drunk every night. Her parents had a lot of problems, with all those kids—never enough money, never enough time. Your grandma did the best she could to hold things together, when grandpa would go away for weeks at a time, to find the only jobs he could get.

And the kids? Well, they too made the best they could of it. There was always plenty of work to do. Confusion and chaos were a constant all around them. But there simply was not enough love and caring to go around. They hid inside themselves, handling things on the surface, feeling alone and forgotten on the inside. Usually, they pretended that the outside was all there was. It helped to make the pain less real. It was the only way their parents knew, and so they learned it too.

Today, we know that this is a very common pattern followed by families where alcoholism or poor parenting is present. But no one knew it then. The importance of knowing is that, until we realize exactly what the pattern is and what we are doing to carry it on, we continue acting in exactly those same limited, self-defeating ways we learned in our families. And we pass the pattern on, from one generation to the next.

Even when the drinking and the drugs are no longer a part of our lives, we still haven't learned any better ways of communicating and relating to each other. Unconsciously, we pass the sickness on. We hide our feelings and our weakness. We act tough and strong—especially when we feel weak and hurt. We never ask for what we want and need; we either do without, or we try to get it in some indirect way. We feel we aren't important, and our needs don't matter, so we shouldn't ask for much.

We sometimes get very angry about this, but it's against our law to tell anyone how we feel. We might blow up at some unrelated little thing. Or, more likely, we take it out on ourselves, putting ourselves down and beating ourselves up. Our self-esteem is miserable; the only time we feel worthwhile is when we're helping someone else.

This is the pattern, Bonita, that your mom, and now you, have grown up with. Fortunately, in our day, some people are learning to heal it. But it's not a learning that comes automatically, so those who don't seek it out may never find it—and may never realize what they're missing or that their lives could be much happier if they did some work on themselves.

Well, I may be all wrong, but I'm guessing that this all may mean something to you, too. I wonder if, as you have been reading this, you have recognized some of these signs in your family. Do they sound familiar to you? If they do, then *you* might be the one in your family who can begin the healing process. I suspect you are already doing this, on your own. How can you do it? Well, there's a lot to learn. But at least, today, there are places to learn it from, and other people who understand.

So when you say, "Nobody looks at my *inside*," my heart goes out to you. But I wonder who in the world would not be able to see the beauty inside you, if you *show* it to them, as you've shown it to me in your letter? What do you think: could you make a tape recording for your mom, telling her how alone you feel and how much you'd like to be able to talk to her? Maybe tell her some of the beautiful thoughts you've shared with me. How wonderful it would be for you, if you could only feel your parents know who you really are, and understand you. You probably still wouldn't agree on all the little points of everyday living, but they wouldn't be so important if better communication can be opened up.

Let me know what you think about all this. And thank you so much for sharing your thoughts with me. You are such a special young lady, I feel very lucky to know you.

> With love,
> Sarah

This writer wrote a feedback note in her journal: "I want to keep in touch. We have many more things to share. I will tell Bonita this, and remain available to her. I'll send her a diary and encourage her to write about her thoughts."

"Wisdom letters" like these demonstrate the use of letter-writing techniques to reach out and support those we care about. Letter writing offers an excellent way of developing our own wisdom and sharing it with others in time of need.

LETTERS OF THANKS

Almost nothing feels as good as expressing our thanks to someone we appreciate and who has made a difference in our lives. The simplest letter can be one we'll want to save forever in our journals.

> Dear Mom and Dad,
>
> I'm sitting here in my new bedroom at the end of a good, productive day, listening to Christmas music . . . and there is something I've been thinking about for quite a while, and that is to write you a thank you letter. I am *so* grateful to have you guys as my parents. There are so many things I look back and remember—simple things I remember taking for granted growing up—the fact that you loved me! I have been astonished over the years to learn of all the women who were abused or mistreated as children (one book I read quoted 45% having been sexually molested [of grown women]). I have *several* friends who had horrible experiences as children—I am so thankful to have been loved!
>
> I am so grateful for your:
> letting me make my own choices and supporting me
> helping with the kids
> planning wonderful holidays
> letters and phone calls filled with news and encouragement
> bringing the Isuzu out for me
> loads of money loans
> providing for Kirk's surgery
> visits
> gifts of furniture, jewelry, silver—wonderful extras!

For all you have done, I thank you!

I am often complimented for my capability, courage and strength—I know where I observed and learned those qualities—and it was at home—from you.

I love who I am—I am happy, whole, healthy and I feel such tremendous joy most of the time and I feel I owe it to your guidance when I was young. I believe I have been a good parent and I believe I learned that from you.

So, for all these, and many other blessings which will go unsaid, I thank you, as we approach this season of great joy and celebration. I celebrate with you and feel exceedingly blessed!

I love you both very much,
Bev

Here is your invitation to start writing letters. If you are already a letter writer, write more. Share your life with those you cherish. Letter writing is one of the highest forms of self-expression. It keeps you in touch with your thoughts and feelings, and by participating with those you love, you become richer. Letter writing is a self-affirmation of the most benevolent kind.

8

Tap Into Your Inner Knowing—
Opening to the Power of the Subconscious

THE UNLIMITED POWER of the subconscious mind resembles the vastness of the heavens. Your subconscious mind knows no restrictions of time and space. Become the voyager and explore your subconscious mind. Astronomers use telescopes to explore the reservoirs of space and see the revelation of the stars. Journal writing is the telescope to explore the universe of our subconscious mind.

The subconscious mind is the home of your deepest, most heartfelt desires. It does your every bidding. It asks no questions and will accept as fact whatever you consider to be true. The subconscious is limitless. It remembers everything you think, feel, say and do, and stores it quickly in perfect order to return it to you exactly as given. It is a humble, efficient servant always eager to create. It speaks in the language of pictures, symbols and images. The subconscious has the ability to tap into unlimited intelligence. This concept is called possibility thinking.

A useful form of possibility thinking in journal writing is achieved through the use of fantasy. The subconscious mind does not know the difference between reality and possibility thinking. I encourage the use of fantasy in journaling as a most effective means of initiating change. Only by practicing and reinforcing a new pattern of thinking can the subconscious be used at its most powerful and effective level. A few great inventors, composers and mystics have been keenly aware of the power of the subconscious, and have harvested great benefits from the use of possibility and fantasy thinking. For me, journeys into fantasy writing can be one of the most direct means of tapping into this possibility thinking, as well as for reaching our potential, and experiencing our joy.

Journaling provides invitation and access to the subconscious mind or your inner knowing. It was not until I started journaling that I realized I had an unlimited wealth of information and resources inside that I could access any time. One of the simplest techniques to use in contacting the subconscious is simply to close your eyes and ask, "What information wants to come through me?" Remain quiet and receptive for a few minutes. Then open your eyes and begin writing your thoughts without any editing.

To encourage your subconscious mind to come forth you may want to create the most fertile, receptive conditions possible. First, find a quiet place where you can be undisturbed and can eliminate possible interruptions. Set aside the time you will need—anywhere from ten or twenty minutes to an entire day or weekend. Put on some of your favorite background music (or relaxation/meditation audio tapes) that will enhance your focus. Candles, incense, or flowers may be used to add ambience.

Make yourself comfortable, in a sitting or lying position, with notebook and pen close at hand, and close your eyes. Taking several deep breaths, allow your body to become calm and relaxed. Imagine that you are stepping into a shallow pool of warm water, or lying in the sun on a beautiful tropical beach. Focus on releasing tension from each part of your body, and on breathing peaceful energy in and out. Invite your mind into a state of inner knowing, allowing any thought to flow past your screen of vision like a cloud moving across the sky.

When you feel totally relaxed and ready, open your eyes and remain "soft-eyed," so that you can begin writing without leaving this state of consciousness. Write any thought or impression that comes into your mind. Record any pictures and images, using drawing or symbols if they occur. Don't try to make logical, intellectual sense of these thoughts, and don't worry about spelling or punctuation. Just record what appears each moment, unedited.

Color Imagery

Imagery in colors—a treelike form from a fairy book with a huge knothole—my sense of something hiding in it—a black buglike creature facing me head-on (a huge creature, frightening *looking* but not scary to me). And then:

- the sensation of green, growth, all kinds of shades of green gradually drifting into . . .
- the image of a fairy, Tinker Bell, lying on her back, arms under her head, feet in the air, leaning against a tree; then
- burnt orange—forming itself into an arm carrying a torch, the sense of light and strength
- then lavender ruffles edged in dark blue, a dancer's skirt
- then red—not a real object; fingers of color like some strange tropical flower
- becomes then a silvery Christmas tree-like object—crystal? A sensation of crystal floating into white and silver. And then . . .
- into rosebushes, not yet in bloom, and then
- a stage and a troop of actors—inviting—what? To watch or be? It's like an audition.
- And the final image: an actor looking like Shakespeare, garbed in gold and white, his arms outstretched—welcoming?

When you feel complete and ready to stop writing, open your eyes and reread your work. Give yourself feedback on it. Your feedback may also not flow logically from this type of writing. Go with your *feeling* about the piece, your hunch about its meaning. Let your intuitive mind speak. What does the piece say to you? What is the essence of the writing? What is the underlying feeling or theme?

Let the *Feedback Statement* choose you. Don't *think* about it, just let it come. The writer of the preceding piece wrote the following feedback on her work.

Feedback: I am in amazement at the strength of the color imagery—surprised at the form of this meditation. I feel excitement at getting closer to my unconscious self, my creative energy. To journal, for me, is to get in touch with the creative, the visionary part of myself. I have the sense of being in touch with untapped power at the source of my being.

NATURE AS YOUR METAPHOR

The energetic, playful spirit of the dolphin-self in you revels in plunging into the waves, and riding the curl of the swirling surf. The free, unencumbered spirit of the seagull in you swoops high into the clouds without a downward glance. The wise owl in you watches and studies every moment, every flicker in the night. The sly fox creeps along in dark shadows as you cautiously size up your best approach. The forever optimistic cocker spaniel in you meets every new opportunity with uncensored glee. You curl up and purr in a pool of sunshine as the sleek, snobbish cat—the world pauses to nap with you.

Nature can be a rich and revealing metaphor for where we seem to be in our lives. Each aspect of nature can be our teacher when we invite forth the metaphor from our subconscious.

I Am Nature

I am like a mountain stream, twisting, churning, bubbling and powerful. Each ripple I feel signifies the life force within me. I am the surge of the constant undercurrents, yet as storms fill me and renew my rushing power, my banks overflow with the new surplus. I want to be like this river—never questioning, always strong on my course, and yet changing as I must in response to "the elements."

The difference between a man-made channel and a natural one lies in the power of nature to be constant yet never changing, twisting and bending to the elements. I need not question "Where is my riverbed to take me next?" but simply go with the flow.

If you close your eyes and ask the question "What in nature am I like?" you may be amazed by the information that comes. Our metaphors are sometimes so close to the surface, they can just leap right out—and we may never realize this until we take the time to write.

The Night Outside

I am outdoors, camping. The sky is pitch black. Sparks fly out from the camp fire, and a cricket chirps in the distance. Tall trees surrounding the campsite reach out to the nearby sky, into whose infinite peace all growing things nestle at night.

I am very much like the dark sky. I have the possibility of infinity, infinite wisdom, knowledge, and love. The sky never asks what it is. God meant this to be true for me, too. I'm sure of it.

Columbines

"I am one of those beautiful columbines that grew near the doorway in soil regularly fertilized by the dairy herd gathered there—gorgeous, huge blossoms, nourished by all the shit I've grown through."

Your image of the moment may be beautiful and expansive, or small and annoying, like the woman who reported, "I hate it. My image is a squirrel. Scurrying here, scurrying there, gathering up my little nuts and hiding them away . . ." Whatever it turns out to be, there is always something valuable to learn from the image and the metaphor.

One of the most powerful images I have ever received came when I once wrote: "I am like a geyser. You can't stop up a geyser." I further realized "Of course you can't stop up a geyser!" I went on to conclude: "I give myself permission to release that incredible force that comes from within."

The strong identity you feel with an image in nature can be tapped from the subconscious to interact with in your journal. Simply ask your image to come forth and teach you.

I Am a Snowflake

I am a snowflake, unique and beautiful. I float down from a soft cloud and gaze down upon the lovely earth. I observe the heavy gray clouds with the rosy pink borders of a sunset. I see the green of the forest, and the purple mountains. I smile at the freedom of the children and animals. I am filled with awe and wonder. I float alongside other snowflakes, joining in their motion without enmeshing together.

When I reach the ground, I feel afraid. Will I melt? Will I be stepped on? Will someone come around and crush me into a snowball? Am I afraid of losing myself?

Feedback: I feel very vulnerable at this time in my life. It's exciting and fun, and I am very alive. But I must keep my vision up off the ground and guard my fragile identity.

By stepping out of our conscious state, we allow our subconscious inner knowing to access the symbols and imagery of universal truth.

ACCESSING YOUR INNER WISDOM

As a small child, I loved to fish with my grandfather in the creek near his farm. "How do you know there are fish in there?" I remember asking him. "First you trust that they're there. Then you put the worm on your hook, you drop him into the water and you can count on those fish being hungry!" Granddad counseled. So it is with accessing inner wisdom. First, you trust that it is there. Wisdom is such a powerful idea. Synonyms for wisdom are knowledge, learning and enlightenment. You have all those within you. Bait yourself with the idea of daydreaming and drop the line to your imagination to feed yourself the guidance you seek.

Einstein, Edison, Franklin and Thoreau were all great daydreamers. When these wise men would come upon a situation to which their logical, rational minds could find no solution, they would relax and daydream, each in their own fashion. Edison would nap and awake with answers. Whatever method you choose, I encourage daydreaming. It is one of the easiest ways to access your inner wisdom. The legacy of accessing inner wisdom is that you dip beneath the analytical surface to the deeper currents of inner truth, awareness and enlightenment.

No Security Inside the Chains

I am in a pool of water. I have a feeling of being weighted down and yet buoyant at the same time. My body feels heavy, yet I can float all day. I float through my life, not truly thinking of the heavy thoughts much. The weights I feel are with me, and I strain to rid myself of them. I am free and I am tied up. I am in chains that I have wrapped around myself for security. But there is no security inside the chains.

Feedback: I am looking at my life with Ken and wondering what I have to do. I am tired of floating. I want to dive deep and swim with my eyes open. I am ready to make a decision.

It is only when the knowledge from our subconscious mind surfaces that we may take conscious action on it.

As we explore the subconscious mind we find that it contains an infinite library of universal truth. When you direct the conscious mind for guidance and information, the wisdom you seek presents itself.

A Place of Light and Color

We are gathered in a place of light and color. Our child selves are in a classroom. We are gathered to learn. A silvery gentle voice says: "The healing of the planet starts with you, as individual child-self and as part of groups and families everywhere who are drawn together to move beneath the surface of life and grow to wholeness.

"You must seek to learn forgiveness for those who, from their own need, their own unknowing child-self, have caused you pain. Seek union and trust with all who cross your path and seek to shift the negative mass consciousness from struggle to peace.

"Healing is a moment-by-moment process. It comes through releasing demands and expectations of others. Healing IS forgiveness.

One journaler told me that she was bored with herself. "What kind of journaling can I do to find out what is fascinating in me?" she asked. I recommended she journal with the parts of her that create mystique.

The Parts of Me

I was seated in a lovely white chair with soft padding, and I invited the others in. Anger arrived first in red and said, "I've been afraid to cross this threshold before, but now I'm here."

Then on my right came Spirit, floating in and enveloping the room in a soft turquoise mist. "I am here to take you through anything and everything that might challenge you."

Next Power entered and took its place in a majestic, throne-like chair. "I am here to serve you at all times. And I will remind you to stand up for who you are."

There was Compassion, green and creeping into the corner, wanting to manipulate my power. He whispered, "I can serve you best as the fusion of power with compassion."

Love entered and went to the center of the table. "I'm here to be visual and visible. I come from your center. I came in with you from the beginning, and I will remain here always."

Last came Passion and immediately asked me to hold her. I became an impassioned soul. I was filled with emotion as I looked around me. I thanked all the parts of me for coming and asked them to continue to serve me to become more intriguing.

Feedback: I embrace all the parts of me. I'm excited about a dialogue with the rest of me.

I knew a young woman whose primary focus was the unfinished work in her house. When she started writing she realized that her real problem was her marriage, and the state of her house was a metaphor for the state of her marriage. Journaling from the place of inner knowing took her beneath surface concerns to the very heart of the matter.

Wasted Drops

I am chasing Max. Running after him, saying, "Open up! Open up!" There he is, painting the new door, changing the leaky faucet. So busy, trying to please me. I'm sure he's doing these things just to make me happy. The door makes me happy. At least for a day. I look at the windowpanes and notice how much brighter the kitchen is . . . then I can't help noticing, beyond that, the rest of the unfinished laundry room. Judging, judging, judging—never enough. Not enough money, not enough projects, not enough time to do what I want.

My life is full of escape. Complain about the leaky faucet or the dirty towels instead of saying, "I feel awful about wasting water and I really feel awful wasting my life." The truth is, I could care less about leaky faucets if my life were filled with love. The wasted drops are like wasted minutes. The drops add up to gallons and the minutes to a lifetime.

Reflection: I'm looking at where I choose to be and what I really want to accomplish in my life. Looking at the overall picture, I have to face it that Max never finished a damn thing in his life. What's really bothering me? That I put up with it. That I'm so disappointed. I'm also looking at the gift of each moment. There are no wasted drops of life—each drop is a gift to be received.

One woman arrived at a journaling class in a state of anger. Her frustration with the organization she worked for prompted the following writing that allowed her inner wisdom to flow.

Woman Warrior

The women were lining the shores of the river. Some were attending busily to their tasks; others stood vacant—or dreamy-eyed. Several watched as the men in canoes floated by.

Suddenly one tall woman spoke out. "No, it is not my destiny to stand on the shore. I am to be the warrior. I can no longer be passive." She set her belongings down and stood tall.

She was free. The other women watched as she walked toward the mountains, frightened and energized by her movement.

Feedback: I do know it is the time for women to lead.

A woman came up to me after a writing exercise designed to put people in touch with their inner knowing. "I didn't get very much from this," she said, perplexed.

"Have you ever done this before?" I asked, and she replied that the whole idea was very new to her.

When you're attempting to open the window and look into your inner knowing, you can't wave a magic wand and expect everything to jump into place in a perfectly ordered picture. This kind of writing experience takes time and patience. With practice, listening within becomes more and more natural. With practice your trust builds, and you find yourself more able to slip in and out of the realm of your deep inner knowing. And with time your inner knowing will reveal more and more of the magic and mystery that is inside of you.

Journaling from your inner knowing is an evolving and unfolding process. It is one you may find yourself doing more of because it's a refreshing *vacation* from the daily processes of the mind—a vacation to bask in and enjoy its gifts.

ACCESSING A DREAM MESSAGE

Dreams can provide us with a gift of truth from the subconscious mind. If you want to unlock the puzzle of who you are, open the treasure chest of swirling internal possibilities, dreams can be one of the portholes to the magic of your life.

To examine and learn from your dreams, try writing out the sequence of the dream as soon as you awake. Record any thoughts or feelings that come up. Read over what you have written. Then write what the dream may be saying to you. Is there a theme, a recurring or underlying thought or feeling? I suggest titling your dreams. Titles provide a means of quickly identifying and organizing important dreams in an accessible memory bank.

In periods of active dreamwork, when you find yourself having frequent meaningful dreams, it is helpful to keep a dream journal. Your subconscious mind may be busy laying the groundwork for your next growth step.

You may not want to log and interpret your dreams on a daily basis, but I strongly suggest paying attention to what I call the "screaming dreams." These are the ones that jump out from your subconscious mind, begging to be looked at.

Sunday Night Dream

The place where I was staying was filled with rats! They had a route which led from my bedroom, where there was a trapdoor in the floor, to an opening in the wall of the kitchen where they could get through to the outside. I hated the rats—they gave me the creeps! There were many people there in the dream with me to help me get rid of the rats, and I seemed to be in charge. I didn't like the idea of killing them. None died in my dream. The babies were darling. I dreamt all night long.

Feedback: I've been sleeping with a rat. The man in my life right now is a rat . . . I see that now! No more rats!

You can use many other techniques to understand and work with your dreams. You might want to write a dialogue between characters or elements of a dream, or write a story that follows up or resolves a dream. When people from your past appear in a dream, it is often valuable to write and answer the question, "What can I learn now from this person who has just reappeared in my dreams?" When there is dream work you would like to do, consider using any of the techniques in the other chapters of this book. For example, employing the conversation technique from Chapter 5 may allow you to find out what the message is to you from the person who appears in your dream.

UNLEASH YOUR IMAGINATION— THE JOY OF PRETENDING

Stories, like dreams, invite us into the joy of discovering and learning. Out of the treasure of our imagination we can tap a fantasy rich in meaning and messages. Some messages are brilliantly obvious and others are hidden behind the gauze curtains of metaphor.

For some, unleashing the imagination is a difficult task. To use the fairy tale, parable or metaphor can be a new and sometimes intimidating experience. To ignite your imagination takes nothing more than giving yourself permission to play and pretend. To invite the parts of you that represent the clown, the actor, the author or the magician, is to treat yourself to your own great adventure.

Take a piece of paper, and at the top draw your version of a suitcase or flight bag. Title your writing, "I am going on a journey to _____." Below list all the things you want to take with you on your imaginary journey. Your list can be unlimited—not confined to clean socks and a toothbrush. Pack a nightingale to accompany you with song. Tuck in a diamond tiara or a gem encrusted scepter, because where you plan to go you will be the ruler—the king or the queen of your new domain. Read over your list, give yourself a *Feedback Statement* and begin writing a make-believe story about your adventure.

Remember, your imagination can go anywhere and do anything, and the domain you create can bring you joy.

Fantasy journaling expands your thinking. Instead of recording reality, it lets you create an entirely new story or script. By blending the real and the unreal, a new level of awareness can unfold for the journaler.

A Journey to Oz

A billow of clouds. I am rushing through the air nearly breathless, propelled by some unforeseen force into the dawn—like Dorothy, I imagine. I surrender into the force, and then I see the yellow brick road, the ruby slippers, and the Emerald City. I skip the bad part (even though I know you can't skip the bad part). There *are* witches in Oz, you know. They sometimes hide in the corners of my mind and I have to muster the strength to confront them before I can see the Emerald City—before I can go home.

I am reminded that the Wizard doesn't *rescue*; he rewards the fearless facing of the challenge. It is through action that the cowardly lion becomes brave. But even though the journey requires solo starts, it is enhanced by munchkin appreciation, fellow travelers, and a good witch to point the way.

Feedback: The child in me understands more than my everyday mind sometimes remembers. And that's fun.

Fantasy writing can take many forms—poetry, short story, stage play or screenplay. You may want to write in myth, science fiction or fairy tale.

Follow the path to the undiscovered. Open the door to the magician's closet. Don't accept that reality is all there is! Be daring, try a new flavor, break out of the mold!

I love to use the expression "Aha!"—the moment when curiosity becomes awareness. In that illuminating instant a revelation occurs, out of which self-healing can often take place.

Princess Phyllis

Once upon a time, there was this princess named Phyllis. She was not one of your pallid princesses who faint at the drop of a crown. If you faint you miss stuff, and Phyllis didn't want to miss anything. She was tough, and smart, and Irish, and had red hair and a freckle or two. When she was little she lived with her mother and father in Og-wog-bedonia.

Og-wog-bedonia has many kingdoms within its borders, and she lived in sort of the northwest part, in the kingdom of Fruitful Plantings. Her mother, Queen Peaches, lived there. The queen was married but I forget her husband's name. (You know how it is in kingdoms; you remember the ruler but not necessarily the spouse.)

Anyway, Princess Phyllis was very happy in this kingdom. She played and sang and fished and wrote stories and dried tree bark and got into mischief (even princesses have to do that from time to time) and generally got stronger every day. She was so strong she could even take care of her invalid sister. Sometimes that meant giving her a hard time and a certain amount of teasing so she could get strong too.

It is a good thing Phyllis got so strong, because one day there was a war in the kingdom. Phyllis lost both parents and she and her sister were rescued by two dumb elves without a map who took them to the kingdom of Trial by Fire. It happens sometimes. Usually people don't get sent there until they are grown-ups, because it is a place others can lead you to but only you can get yourself out of. This is hard for children, because they are small and usually not allowed to travel by themselves.

The kingdom of Trial by Fire is not a happy place. The scenery can be nice, but that's about it. The grown-ups who run it are mean and selfish and insensitive. They shout and hit and order everyone around and drink too much. In their eyes, nothing you ever do is good enough, and they don't believe in play. It is a place where you have to hide your dreams in jars like fireflies and keep them alive by yourself without help, lots of times. You have to say your own special magic words to keep from being cast permanently under the spell of the wicked witches and warlocks who keep saying you are stupid or ugly or a worm or whatever. Sometimes you have to hold so tight to the knowledge of who you really are—a royal prince or princess—that your fingers hurt.

But Phyllis held on, no matter how sad she got. She knew who she was because of her beginnings in Fruitful Plantings, which was a good thing since she and her sister were sent to live with a real dragon. This creature had taken parenting classes from Cinderella's stepmother. Phyllis also knew that as long as she resisted the fire that wanted to shrivel her and dry her up, she'd be okay even if smoke got in her eyes.

Now part of the reason she knew this was because there was this little voice inside her head. You know, it's that little something that tells you, "I didn't do anything wrong," when other people are ranting and raving and ordering you about. Well, she didn't know it at the time, but there was this little invisible munchkin named Manzanitas protecting her.

You see, the Imperial Og, who ruled the whole land, had a very large battalion of trained elves, dwarves, angels, and fairies that he would send into Trial by Fire as personal bodyguards. (It doesn't matter if you believe in them or not, if you listen you can hear them. It's real hard to see them because they know you might tell, and then people will say you are crazy and maybe send you to the Booby Hatch, which is even harder to get out of than Trial by Fire!)

The Imperial Og knew that Phyllis had the potential to be one of the Superbeings who live in the land of Light That Sparkles. Those are the people who are so strong inside that they can take care not only of themselves and their sisters, but also of other children and women and men. That's why he sent Manzanitas, who was one of his favorites.

Manzanitas didn't help out much with the work. He was more of an idea man. He had little idea eggs that he hatched for Phyllis whenever things got quiet. His most memorable ideas had to do with ways to destroy the parenting dragons. (These ideas gave Phyllis a lot of comfort, even though she knew she wouldn't stoop to their level and act on them.) He also nudged Phyllis in her ear and told her to sneak outside and go play stick ball in the alley.

And so the years went by as they do. Phyllis grew stronger

every day and Manzanitas grew wittier. (He always did love a good laugh.) The Imperial Og was pleased as well as relieved when Phyllis was old enough to escape with Manz, and did. (Not everyone realizes it's possible to listen to spirits and move out of Trial by Fire. Some people stay there forever. They forget about Light That Sparkles. Hard to believe in this age of air travel, but nevertheless true.)

Phyllis knew her days in Trial by Fire were over, so she set out to travel the world and reclaim her power. She visited many famous places, like Marriage Mountain, Motherhood Manor, Corporate Creations, and Mixed Media, and then she began to write about them. Manz helped her remember the details. He was tickled pink, and other colors, as he watched the light of her Superbeing self grow to diamond-bright brilliance.

Then one day she began to see it too. She finally realized someplace deep inside that people weren't just being nice or polite or well behaved when they said they loved her or that her words moved them or that they no longer felt so alone in the world when they heard her stories. She had always been powerful, but now she finally knew it.

Today Phyllis lives in the land of Light That Sparkles, where she is known as Queen of Fruitful Plantings and Woman Who Heals with Her Heart.

Manzanitas still keeps her company, just for the fun of it!

"Just for the fun of it" turned out to be the gift of this writing which affected two people: the journal writer and the woman about whom it was written. One was empowered by the sheer force of creativity and imagination. The other was deeply touched by the power of the story about herself. In the same way that magic delights and goes beyond the limits of our minds, journal writing can take you to the untouched realms of joy and creative expression.

The following imaginative short story was written by a woman experiencing significant mood swings in her life. This writing allowed her to sort out her thoughts and emotions, as well as discover what is really important to her now.

Racing Silks

In the jockey's room at the track is a wall filled with racing silks—bright, shiny shirts, every hue of nature, hanging carefully on hooks along the wall beneath the owners' labels. How shall I choose?

By color?

By owner?

By bloodline?

What if I were to pick my silks for today by *spirit,* instead? So many colors, so vivid, can dull the vision and numb the senses; choosing becomes the task of catching a kaleidoscope pattern as it spins in a frenzy.

I close my eyes and let my spirit of today catch the gray or the gold, the purple or scarlet, the green or white. What raiment will I don? What steed will I mount and hold tightly reined at the starting gate?

The color of my shirt determines the owner, and the owner determines the horse, and the horse determines the race.

My spirit today is jaded and weary, and I reach for a shirt of gray, trimmed with dull green sleeves and yoke. Above the empty hook, as I fasten the buttons, I read the owner's name: "Overwork Farms." I head for the paddock to find my mount. There, against the railing, stands a handsome triple crown winner of years past, alert, head high, nostrils flared, eyes bright in anticipation; a thoroughbred of impeccable breeding, slightly older than the rest of the field. I am hoisted into the saddle and head to the gate, astride this horse called "Driven."

I may win today. I may not.

Another day my joyful spirit reaches for the scarlet and gold, its companion colors; and the legend over the hook reads: Owner —New Life Stables. When I check for the "New Life" entry in today's race, I discover a frisky, black-maned entry named "Exultation," and, as I lead this incredible animal out of the paddock, I know in every fiber of my being that I wear the winning colors today and that the horse and I will last the race this time and many more to come. And we shall break records and know the heady smell of roses, and thrill to the noisy celebrations round about as we grasp the cup and hold it high.

Another time, when my spirit is an undistinguishable pattern of confusion and hurt, I look for the worn hook at the end of the wall and take down a shirt of faded blues and dark reds, with sweat stains on the collar, under the arms, and in the small of the back. The owner's name for these silks is "Heart's Acres," and the horse I mount has been ridden by many before me.

We start the race in a spurt and quickly lead the field, yet before long this thoroughbred, with a registry that has been questioned by many judges over the years, who is listed in the daily Tip Sheet as "Frustration," sired by "Negative," born of "Reaction," becomes distracted and seems to forget the purpose of the race. We lose the lead, making many strategic mistakes, and, concentration broken, we quickly fall back.

It is hard to beat the oddsmakers when you are riding "Frustration."

When you have ridden enough races, you have worn most of the silks on the wall and you have raced on the backs of almost every spirit horse in the paddock.

I am the jockey and it is my spirit which chooses—colors, owners, studs.

Let me choose winning colors again, for I like the smell of roses, the feel of the gold metal as I lift the winner's cup. And my mount and I are one, united in the celebration of the crowds, made richer by our race.

To get out of an emotional or mental rut, journalers can write poems titled according to their desired action or result. Close your eyes and let your imagination soar.

Flight Uniform

Marked down
Picked over
Taken off the rack
Put in a brown paper bag.

Take home
Make do
Open up the sack
Hang on a big wooden hook.

Shower cap
Green soap
Water from the spout
Dry me off on a thick, pink towel.

Eyes wide
Lips red
Lotion on the feet
Silk slides smoothly over my head.

What's this?
Old dress?
Magic really happens
What was old is now brand-new.

Colors bright
Dazzling sight
Diamonds from the vault.
These must be my flying clothes.

A friend of mine was considering going into counseling. He wrote a parable to delve deeply into his own being hoping to see what was at the root of his dissatisfaction, and if counseling would be the next step for him.

Disconnected Buttons

Susan and I are still in the middle of an ongoing discussion about emotional buttons, or the hypothetical connection between external events and internal feelings. I feel disconnected with Susan as though I've let go of something.

The image that comes to mind is of someone who habitually carried a large parcel in his arms and refused to put it down to embrace people. Finally one day, he tripped over a crack in the sidewalk and the package fell from his grasp. As luck would have it, the package was crushed under the wheels of a passing truck. He was terribly upset by the loss of the package, for in it he carried all his hopes and desires. And so he sat down and stared at his crushed package. He felt outraged. That crack in the sidewalk was to blame. The truck driver was to blame. His anger grew.

Pretty soon his anger was so out of control that he decided to put it in a box. Now he once again had something to carry with him. The box was heavy. Instead of carrying it in his arms, he got a handtruck to help him lug it around, for he was afraid to let it out of his sight. He had lost one box before from carelessness, and he was not going to let it happen again. His life was centered around the box. He changed the way he did things to accommodate the box. He bought two seats on airplanes. He bought a pickup truck instead of a motorcycle. He never ate at nice restaurants since head waiters were snooty about people with large parcels. Eventually he lost his job over the box.

Support groups had not yet been organized for his particular malady. He became a streetperson, jobless, friendless, hopeless, angry and frustrated—and yet he held even more tightly to the box. One night he dreamed he was walking on the beach and he had no clothes. Now that was not what really bothered him—it was that his cherished box was gone!

Night after night, this terrible dream became a recurring nightmare, until . . . One morning when he woke up, the fear and anxiety of the missing box became a dreaded reality. His box had been stolen. He spotted the garbage truck just rounding the corner, and then he heard a crushing sound as the compactor smashed his box of anger flat, just as his box of hope had been flattened by the wheels of a truck. Now he had nothing. No hope, no desire, no anger. What was left? He decided to set out in search of a box that was indestructible in which to store his despair.

At that moment Joy came dancing up the street. She was so delightful, he was drawn irresistibly to her brightness and energy. Never before had he imagined such a Being existed. Enlightenment was new to him. He tried to get Joy to live in a box so he could carry her with him always. Joy was not content to live in a box like anger and despair. Joy had a life all her own and wanted to get out and meet people and rustle among all the emotions of life.

He and Joy spent hours together talking, laughing, creating. Joy told him the truth. The truth pushed his buttons. He often got angry or frustrated with Joy. And yet, Joy remained his friend. Joy was not like the others. They would lie to him to appease his anger. Joy had no attachment to what his reactions were. Joy was wise in the ways of emotional buttons. Joy knew that the truth would evoke his anger, and still Joy spoke the truth with no fear, for Joy knew the truth about buttons!

Feedback: The truth about buttons is that other people don't push my buttons . . . I push them myself. And the black box method is a very burdensome and ineffectual way of trying to keep my feelings under control. Look to Joy, and tell the truth about your feelings.

My friend gained the confidence to proceed with counseling because he had a grasp of his truth. After completing this highly creative and illuminative piece, the writer also came to the conclusion that he had all the information inside to make the necessary decisions and changes in his life.

Committed journalers learn to turn to their journals to answer questions for themselves. It is a valuable technique and practice to enhance working with a therapist, or trusting yourself for guidance.

I often encourage my clients to write a story when they are feeling lost or stuck and unable to see the light at the end of the tunnel. It often allows their subconscious mind to surface to identify the problem and create a solution. It also serves to free them from over analyzing, and "thinking" out their problems too much.

The Grandfathers

I see a pathway—some trees—a black cat, and then the Indian village. The grandfathers' medicine wheel. Seeking wisdom, I find the tent of the grandfather of the north—the speaker to me of the peace within—of silent spaces and a heart that loves the thunder. His message is acceptance: Let the winds of sadness wash over you and blow past. They will not linger if you do not try to hold them or to ride the wind.

My grandfather of the east, resplendent in cape and crown of eagle feathers, bearing the eagle like a falcon, is angered. It is the repetition, he says. You know the light needs dark to illumine most radiantly. You must learn acceptance of the way of the living world. The eagle's soaring has no meaning to him except in contrast to the moments of stillness. Seek the grandfather of the south. Return to the child self.

The grandfather of the south wears green and is engrossed in playing with his mice. He seems more Irish elf than Indian chief. Become your own good parent; allow the child which is you to flow from mood to mood, moment to moment. Do not carry one day past the sleep that leads to the next.

He fades away and is replaced by the grandfather of the west —who, for today, is garbed in sky-blue doeskin. You have the gift of introspection, but you must not misuse its power by finding fault. Look within for truth—not seeking problems, not seeking justification. I look within you and see the wounded healer— and caution patience. You have come far, but deep wounds require time to heal. Don't irritate tender spots, or knock the scabs off. Sometimes resting in the space between the lines will help the healing more than active medicine.

Feedback: Peace, acceptance, patience, going with the flow allow my healing to proceed.

The power of your subconscious is limitless! Possibility thinking, dreams, fantasy and higher-self wisdom have all been explored as resources to tap your inner knowing and expand your joy-filled states of awareness. Try them in your own journal to go beyond where you have never before dreamed possible!

9

The Magic of Writing in a Group

FROM MY very first experience of writing in a group, I was hooked. It was magical. It was like being in an impromptu drama that unfolded right on the spot. People gathered to develop their individual roles and plots which played themselves out in the theater of the whole. The audience was both playwright and players. Writers brought their life scripts to the group and rehearsed their tragedies and fantasies on the stage. Each writer's work was touched and shaped by the work of others. Each person's learning was every person's learning.

While participating in a journaling group new awareness awakened in me. I realized that by consciously observing myself, as well as by observing how others observed themselves, I could make more responsible, effective decisions and determine my life on a higher level of choice. Each emotion someone shared sparked a tie with my own feelings, putting me in touch with times I had experienced comparable situations. It drew out my awareness of the universality of the growth process we all share.

From one person, the journal magic pulled a wrenching story of child abuse. From another popped out a long repressed puppet of playfulness, freed by the release of the abused child. An older man waved a magic wand—or was it a pen?—and suddenly created himself "good enough" for the first time in his life. "My life is my choice!" another woman exclaimed. "If you all can write your lives differently, I know I can write a new career for myself." All these people were in very different places in their lives, yet each had something to learn from the others. As one woman succinctly stated, "We're all on different pages of the same book."

A teenage girl in one group I led said to an older woman, "When I walked in here, you could never have made me believe you had anything to say to me. Now I want to thank you. I see we are in exactly the same place, and your sharing meant so much to me." In a group, the writer's voice in all of us comes out. The synergy of a group deepens the work and empowers the individual.

Now

Now is a blank page
Waiting for its future
New words for old memories
Safely sounded
When friends listen lovingly

THE LISTENER'S ROLE

A listener's role in a journaling group is a simple and special one: *allowing, accepting,* and *being.* Ask yourself, "If that were my work, what would it say to me?" Notice your internal reactions as someone reads aloud their work, and ask, "What is this person's work inviting me to think about?" "What is *my* work in relation to this issue?" Every time someone shares, *it is your work.* Drawing from other people's work is a wonderful way to generate further writing for yourself.

"But I was never a victim of a crime," you might think, trying to make a connection with how one woman's story might relate to yours. And then, exploring more deeply, you might search in your experience for times you have felt violated, or extremely fearful, or when you had difficulty identifying with what someone else was feeling. Do you feel what the person who shares is feeling? If so, what connection have you made? What is there for you to learn? What are you invited to write about? If not, what *do* you feel? What does that tell you about yourself in this moment?

It's a natural temptation as a listener to take a more active role—to give good suggestions, advise the reader based on your experience, or give a thoughtful critique of the work. When we hear someone's story we often want to offer consolation, support, or friendship. But, this kind of participation can actually be more harmful in a journaling group. In becoming "helpers" eager to solve the journal reader's problem, the reader is denied the integrity of owning and resolving their own work. The reader's work and the reader's life are their own. Others may think they know the story from the inside out, but their perceptions are subjective. The journal reader may feel that their privacy has been violated because their reading was not for the purpose of soliciting ideas and feedback. When the listener is working on others they are no longer using the group to work on themselves.

It is not the purpose of a journaling group to take responsibility for anyone else's work. I have found that allowing a journaling group to deviate into "group therapy" can be detrimental to the participants who are exposing their feelings and vulnerability. Most of us are not therapists or professionals who have been specially trained and educated in the complex skills necessary to direct such a group.

The wise educator says to the budding young artist who comes up to show off his work: "Oh, is this your painting? Tell me about it." You know that to respond, "Oh, what a beautiful painting!" would be detrimental to the artistic process. They don't want the child to look to them to judge his work, and to come to depend on their praise or evaluation. They simply listen with interest as he grows in his ability to express himself and to create.

In the journaling groups I facilitate, no one has permission to get into another person's work or to play authority figure. Each person's learning is honored and respected. When this rule is strictly observed, the group can then establish a completely safe atmosphere for all to write and share freely.

SHARING IN A GROUP

I was brought up to be a very private person. It was unthinkable for me to share what I was feeling with anyone. I was to keep things to myself, and not bother anyone else with whatever I was feeling. The result of such conditioning is a sense of being "detached" in the world, even losing touch with what is real inside, and coming to believe that the outer reality is more real and important than the "unacceptable" inner reality.

In writing and sharing your inner world in a non-judgmental journaling group, you can learn to accept and own your inner world. It is okay to write about hating your mother as a child. The group's response is not: "That's terrible!" or, "You poor thing!" but simply acknowledgment and acceptance of you.

It is very freeing to share your writing in such a setting. You can take off your mask—safely. You can let down your guard, and be you. People often say, "It was the sharing, even more than the writing, that brought release. In reading my work out loud, it was as if I heard it for the first time. I *felt* it for the first time. I let my feelings out. It was a huge relief."

Sharing out loud can have powerful results. I have seen long-standing physical symptoms caused by the stress of holding feelings inside and the bottling up of unsaid words, relieved and healed. Life-changing realizations often come out: "I never knew other people have felt these feelings, too. I *can* relate to others in a deeply personal way. I no longer feel separate, strange and isolated. I have shown my worst weakness, and I have not been rejected but accepted for who I am. I cried out, and I was heard. I let myself be known, and I felt supported."

Unjudged Singing Is Most Joyful

Now, once again, I marvel how our separated worlds unite us as one to another in this open heart space of love and gentleness and joy. You know, we're blessed to have this soul space to sing our songs to each other, knowing each song is ours no matter which one of us sings it. . . . Unjudged singing is most joyful. Let's sing chorales 'til Kingdom come!

Another important safeguard for safe sharing in a group is maintaining confidentiality. People will only feel free to share if they can be sure their privacy is honored as a sacred trust. The group should agree that whatever is shared will remain within the group, and never to disclose others' private information to anyone outside the group.

SHARING THE DARK SIDE

"Don't air your dirty laundry," many of us have learned. "Put on a happy face." "Big boys don't cry." "Keep smiling." "Grin and bear it." In a journaling group, the superficial is tossed aside, and we can dare to be ourselves and tell the truth.

One cold, black night a group of journalers sat by a cozy fire watching the sea through a magnificent picture window. The evening's sharing had been universally dark and heavy. Suddenly the windowpane was spattered by wind-blown droppings from a visiting seagull. "How appropriate!" someone said. "This has been a night to 'share the shit'."

It was a relief to know that we could air our dark, painful, terrible experiences and thoughts without losing touch with our sense of group connection, humor and joy. It was clear that sharing the heaviness did not have to drag us down—because we chose to focus on the learning and the value to be taken from it. From that time on, we joked about "sharing the shit" sessions. Whenever the darkness came up, it was an opportunity to shine the light.

Ways to Join Together

Try as I may to be profound
All I can think is
My need to say
Hey, Mom, would you
Go scare Hazel?
Shake her up in
The space between times
So that next time around
She won't torment little children?

Or perhaps in your best Gunston Hall manner
You could say that's not appropriate.
In the meantime
I will think about the ode to a scratchy coat
And ways to join together
To help friends destroy witches

Once and for all—
With an army of words
To accomplish a bloodless coup
That then creates the space
For noble forgiveness
And joyous singing.

STARTING YOUR OWN JOURNALING GROUP

You may find people among your friends and acquaintances, in your neighborhood, school, church, family, place of work, club, or organization who will be interested in meeting together to journal. There is no perfect number of people in a group, and I have always noted that wonderful work can be done no matter how many people are writing together. I have found that six people is a good number to begin with. But I am not disappointed if only five—or two—show up. You can still do the work you have decided to do.

The place your Journal Group meets will be important. It should be private, quiet and separate from interruptions of home or work. There should be enough room for people to spread out in their own cocoon of personal space.

Your group can meet two to three hours at a time once a week, or twice a month. How long your journaling group meets is up to the members and their needs. Some groups meet regularly on an ongoing basis for several months, others for several years. I have observed that new journalers often need at least six meetings to gain an appreciation of the group process and the possibilities of journaling.

HOW A GROUP SESSION WORKS

A definite, regular time for beginning and ending the Journal Group meetings should be observed. They should include a quiet time for writing followed by a sharing session. Meetings should be exclusively for journaling. If members like to engage in conversations and socialize, a special time can be planned for this before or after meetings.

Members of groups sometimes joke about the seemingly strange expectation that they "come in, sit down, and silently write." But they soon grow comfortable with the quiet welcoming smiles they receive, and are freed from any necessity to be there for any other purpose than to write.

I often open a journal group session by inviting everyone to become quiet, close their eyes, and ask themselves, "Where am I in my life right now?" Other times I begin by asking people to write a letter to themselves; or "write out the scatter" in which they pour out their uncensored thoughts onto paper, releasing the load, confusion and stress of the day. Twenty to thirty minutes is given for this initial writing, followed by twenty minutes of coming together to share.

The beginning of each opening sharing session is a good time to review the ground rules for being in the group. Everyone should be aware of these rules and understand their importance as a basis for openness and freedom of expression. It is up to each member to assist in implementing them. Committing to keep the rules is an absolute requirement for staying and participating in the group.

A sharing session can begin by asking, "Who would like to read his or her work?" or by someone offering, "I'd like to share my work." A timer is a good way of keeping everyone on task. When the bell rings after twenty minutes of sharing, it is time to begin writing again. People may want to select some assignment from this book to write about, or choose any subject they are currently dealing with in their lives. Some may prefer to simply sit quietly until an idea inspires them to write, or to do some exploratory writing until they get a clearer sense of what "needs to be written." People should always feel free to move quietly about, go to the bathroom, or get something to drink if they like. They are also free, if they choose, not to write.

The second writing session is timed for twenty or thirty minutes. A few minutes should be set aside for participants to reread their work and write a *Feedback Statement*. Then they can come together again for another twenty minutes of group sharing. (The length of writing and sharing periods may, of course, be adjusted to meet the needs of an individual group.)

To wrap up the meeting, you can take about ten minutes to write a "song of yourself," a poem, or just a sentence or two to bring closure to the journal writing experience. The end of each Journaling Group meeting has its own unique essence. Journalers often write profoundly simple peaceful and joyful pieces like those contained in this chapter. Five minutes for sharing this work concludes the session.

Each for the Other

Can you hear them?
The fairies, circled arm in arm
Are singing Joy to the World
And the child inside each of us
Joins in as heaven's signature sings
And my inner child
Skips around the room
Blowing kisses to everyone
For telling my favorite kind of stories
Stories from the heart
Stories that log our growth
Each for the other and ourselves
In this place of warmth and love and light.

FACILITATING JOURNAL GROUPS

If the group is to have a recognized leader, this person is more of a facilitator and time manager, allowing all group members to retain complete authority over their work and learning. Facilitating a group is not a teaching position, where the person assumes, "I know, and you don't know, so I will teach you." The facilitator, instead, takes charge of convening the meeting and managing its pacing and flow, making sure the ground rules are observed.

As a trained, experienced facilitator, I will sometimes draw out similarities in the work members have done. As it is appropriate I will also guide journalers toward a higher level of integration in their work, and suggest further writing and different perspectives to pursue. For those interested in acquiring training to become a skilled facilitator, information is provided at the back of this book.

Journaling is a gentle, step-by-step, individual process. It is not meant to be highly confrontational, shaking out and forcing the learning that others may see for someone. Learning unfolds naturally when group members each examine and rethink their own work and their own lives. And most importantly, learning is shared by all who listen and make it their own.

Now I Am the Rainbow Arch

Now I am the rainbow arch
And underneath my ephemeral essence
Floats the smiling child of Phyllis
Holding proud her peachy prize
And Donna skips hand-in-hand
With wonders, and John
And Marsha and Barbara, four-year-olds
All run laughing, singing
Gathering the dreams
That Joyce scatters
Like rosebuds from her
Beribboned basket.
God smiles and is not hiding.
It is the hour of enchantment.

10

Celebrate Your Life—
Actualize Your Dreams

> Whatever you can do or dream you can
> do, begin it. Boldness has genuine power
> and magic in it.
>
> —Goethe

NOW THAT YOU have journaled to know who you really are and your passions, how do you want to give back to life? As you find your truth and reclaim your dreams, your journal can empower you to take total responsibility for your life. That's right. You are responsible for deciding what and how you make a contribution to your work place, family, community, or the planet.

ACCENTUATE THE POSITIVE

You must be the star of your own story. Your life choices are your responsibility! You must motivate yourself to decide how you want to live and then move forward with determination. Choose to do it now —and choose to do it with joy!

It is a rare individual who takes the time to record the joy. How many of us sit down to analyze why good things happen? Have you ever had a glorious day, gone home and examined why it was such a good day? How did you create it to be so good?

Most people only take the time to question, analyze, dissect and recreate over and over again in their minds why bad things happen. "How could this have happened? What did I do to deserve this? Where did I go wrong?" Just think how much more powerful and promising an accentuation of the positive is! What do you think would happen in your life if you spent twice as much time focusing on and writing about the good? Want to try? What do you have to lose?

Joy Is Life's Kaleidoscope

It was an especially difficult climb up the face of Cuchuma this morning. I kept stopping to catch my breath and looking back at the magnificent sunrise. The dawn was awash in pinks, blues, and grays. The colors soaked into the morning canvas and extended their warmth over the eastern horizon. Witnessing the beauty and simplicity of this daily recurring event, I was filled with joy. On the way down the back side of the mountain, these thoughts flowed through my mind.

Joy is life's kaleidoscope. It radiates into splendid dimensions at the most unexpected moments. The combinations that formulate joy are as unassuming as the shards of glass that piece together the wondrous design in the magical toy cylinder of the kaleidoscope.

Writing has always been a methodical task for me, time-consuming and tedious. Four hours of scratching out and revising to accomplish ten minutes of still-imperfect narrative. Today I feel as if I have been given a gift. The words just flowed into my consciousness. It matters little whether the gift is to be experienced for ten minutes today and perhaps never again. I am exhilarated that it happened!

Write to appreciate and express your joy more fully. When you feel the warm glow of simple pleasures, or wild and ecstatic happiness, cherish and record these times. Allow yourself to feel deeply. Express your feelings by writing about them in rich, colorful, and joyful detail.

I Would Rather Wear Joy

Sometimes you get so used to depression
It becomes a comfortable thing

Something to wear
Like a comfy old tattered black shawl.

But now it's time for new clothes.
I would rather wear joy
As a crystal cape,
Or eagle feather wings
To soar with the angels
And see the face of God.

THE IMPORTANCE OF BEING AWAKE

Most people are only awake when they have an integrated experience, or one in which all their faculties, mind, body and spirit, are involved. Consider the worst and the best things that ever happened to you. You probably remember every single detail of the experience because every part of you was awake and involved. You recall what you were wearing, how you felt, every word that was said, or not said. You were awake. Being awake is the ability to see clearly through the window of your true self, your soul. A lot of people walk around with the drapes closed on the window of their soul. They may experience brief periods when their drapes are opened and they are awake temporarily, and then go back to a dimly lit perception. Leave the drapes open! In fact, take the drapes off the window altogether, get a bottle of window cleaner and make those windows clear and sparkling.

What Does My Intuition Tell Me?

I'm starting to really look at the people in my life. It would be better to be alone than to have a bunch of toxic people around me. What should I do? None of us is perfect. You have to be tolerant or there will be nobody.

The question is, do I enjoy being around you now? My enjoyment, I realize, comes from talking to (or is it at?) you about your problems. Talk, talk, talk, that doesn't seem to make much difference. Does it serve the bigger picture? Does it help you grow? I can't live your life for you. Does it do me any good either, really? What does my intuition tell me?

I am just pleasuring my ego by getting you to listen to me. My input might make a difference, *if* you asked me and invited it. But my habit is volunteering too much information uninvited. That's my learning—to stay more aware of what it is I want, really want, and not sell out for artificial, ego-gratifying substitutes.

Decide how you want to live. Determine every facet of the life you want to be living. Where do you want to live? Who do you want your friends to be? How do you want to express yourself? Look into the window of your soul and tell yourself the total truth. This writing, all the writing you ever do is for yourself. Remember you are the star! You are in charge. It may take some time and writing to work through the layers of old beliefs and patterns; keep cleaning that window and continue to write. The secret is to become your own authority and teacher, and to keep your focus on the joy!

You Are Your Own Teacher

People seem to need someone outside themselves to look up to for guidance and counsel. The issue of advisors has been troubling me lately, because here I've done it again—I've looked up to and admired Ted, and I am dismayed at what I now see him doing. Why do I seek approval and leadership from others? Why do others do this, too?

I can think of many teachers from history—Caesar, Napoleon, King Arthur, Hitler, Gandhi—and many more who are looked upon as lesser teachers today: bosses, heads of state, fathers, mothers —all authority figures. The potential for abuse is always there when people turn over responsibility for themselves to an outsider.

I just had a flash: *You are your own teacher.* Why does it bother me that people look to others to give them their answers? Because we look to others when we deny that we are our own teacher, if we falsely believe that we are helpless and in need of someone else to show us the way because we can't know it for ourselves —and this is what I have done.

If you don't *need* a teacher, you probably won't be damaged by one. I put Ted above me. I worshiped and adored him. I needed him to be fearless, secure, confident, wise—all the qualities I felt I lacked. This made me vulnerable to being taken advantage of. It made him pretend to be more fearless and wise than he really was, and it made me want to believe so much in him that reality was distorted. From now on, I will simply allow the authority figures to be, and walk around them on the path *I* have chosen. I will decide for myself what I want to do. It's time for me to be my own authority figure. I will design my own curriculum.

SELF-HEALING

What are you feeling right now? Most of us have been trained to be obedient, judgmental and complacent or emotional scorekeepers. Ask yourself: "Am I feeling anger, fear, pain, tension, stress, frustration, sadness, disappointment, resentment?" Being aware of what you are feeling is the first step to self-healing. Is this a feeling state you choose? If the answer is no, pick up your pen and ask yourself a question to begin the healing such as : "When were you first aware of this feeling?"

Let It Out and Let It Go

After writing for half an hour, I feel worse than ever. I'm starting to feel sorry for myself. I am angry, insecure, and very upset. Writing is supposed to shift my energy by getting stuff out of me. Right now I feel like I'm *choking* on stuff. What do I do with all my anger? Am I going crazy? What is going on? I feel yucky and tense and scared right now. I feel pain. It hurts.

What do I do now? What do I want now? I want beautiful, sweet things to come out of me. My writing has become twisted and sick. Nasty, foul-smelling shit is coming out. I feel compelled to keep writing until I am spent. I don't want this nastiness to stay in me.

My writing has taken me into the pit of my own personal hell. It is black and sticky and cold and lonely. I feel desperate and frightened and out of control. Why am I afraid? What have I tapped into?

God, let it out. Whatever it is. My biggest fear. The thing that keeps me stuck. I am purging myself of everything that isn't love, and it is messing up this paper.

Jack is fine. This has nothing to do with him, you know that. It's all you. It is your poison you are spewing out, not Jack's. Keep writing until there's no more.

I feel terror in my gut. Why? I don't know. I guess I need to trust the process. I feel the tears welling up now. What is all this shit? I feel so afraid and alone. So cold. God, show me what writing will really do. Help me to release this pain.

Something special and magical is happening to you. You are cleansing yourself completely of old painful garbage that you have buried deep in your gut. This is going to free you to finally be all of who you are.

Let it out and let it go. Let it go now. Let the fear go. Let the pain go. Let the pain go and let the tears flow. Let the pain move through you; you will be OK. You won't die. Let it roll through you. Go with it. Allow the tears to wash you clean.

Pain is washing and cleansing all your old wounds. They are healing over now, leaving no more sign of injury. You are being born anew—a new creation. You are a person capable of creating warmth in her body just by closing your eyes and thinking warm. Try it. Close your eyes, and be warm . . .

Feedback: I'm still here. I got in touch with a lot of pain. It seems less now. I will continue the process until it is all out. Until it passes out of my body now FOREVER.

The value of this type of writing is that it allows the journaler to write until they identify the feelings and release what is unhealthy and destructive. It is another wonderful example of the cleansing and healing that come through the use of journaling.

Anger Can Eat Holes in Your Soul

No word comes through.
Instead, the idea of a surgical procedure
Lancing a boil
Cutting out a growth

The sense, somehow, that the anger
And whoever the in-my-head voice
Of "not good enough" is
Are linked and must be released,
Cut out, healed, washed clean—
Before I can flow forward with grace and EASE.

Anger can eat holes in your soul
To say nothing of what the acid does to your stomach.

The most lasting healing you can achieve is the healing you give yourself. Listen to your feelings, for their movement through your soul becomes a dance. Once you learn the dance you will have the grace and flexibility to follow or take the lead.

I Will Teach You to Dance

You came in when I was not expecting you.
Perhaps I left a window open when I went to bed,
Although I don't remember doing that.
When I awoke, your tiny black particles
Had sifted all over my normally blithe spirit.
I could not find my dust broom and whisk you away
As I usually do when you sneak in like this.

You have a name, but I do not know your tribe.
You are called sadness, and I think
You are probably related to loneliness and bereavement.

But I divorced all of you a long time ago.
So why are you here, making me so unhappy?
You haven't been invited to my party,
And I want you to go home.
Go away.
My spirit does not look good in black soot.
It dulls the shine.
You had better get going.
For if you don't, I will teach you to dance
And to fly over rainbows.

Victor Frank, author of MAN'S SEARCH FOR MEANING, and a survivor of Auschwitz and Dachau, wrote: "Everything can be taken from a man but one thing: the last of the human freedoms—to choose one's attitude in any given set of circumstances, to choose one's own way."

Your journal is one of the safest and most receptive places to heal your spirit in the light of risk and revelation. In your journal you are free to express the heights and depths of who you are, and to allow your truth to emerge, unconcerned with what others may think or feel.

All I Ever Wanted

Dad, I'm still not clear about my relationship to you. I wish you had been the kind of father I could trust, who would be there for me, be supportive, protect me and (tears) hold me safely in your arms. I never got to be your little girl. You were never there, and I feel a deep sadness about that.

I still wish I had had a daddy like other girls, one who played with me and was happy and fun to be with. One who wanted to have me around. You never did things with me and Alicia for fun. You were either working or going hunting, or out with your friends. You always ran off to do whatever you wanted. You never asked me what I wanted. You always said no to everything I asked.

I'm angry, Dad. I never mattered to you. Yet you wanted me to give you a kiss when you asked. You are attracted to me sexually, which made me so uncomfortable. Didn't you know that's not the way to relate to a little girl? I didn't feel safe around you. I'm still feeling unsafe around men, fearing that if I let myself get too close, they will leave me or use me. I'm still feeling the loss of your love.

I'm so angry that I missed out on having a loving relationship with you. There must be something wrong with me, I concluded, if my own father acts like this to me. So many years of my life were tainted with this awful suspicion. Our lousy relationship has affected me all of my life, and I'm angry about that.

You said we should go to church, but you never went to

church with me. You didn't even believe in God. You are hateful to people of other races. I lost respect for you a long time ago. I don't know if I *ever* respected you.

I'm angry that my children never had a grandfather. I'm angry that you were never supportive of me. You have done nothing but complain about your life or your wife, or my mother—everybody did it to ya, Dad. You are such a helpless wimp, an absolute victim. You put out so much negativity, and you expect love to come back to you. Don't you know that you have to love to be loved!

You don't know how to love. I'm angry because you were the example of male relationships for me. I've been so afraid to get close to a man again. I don't want to be hurt or left again. I deserve better than that, Dad. I deserve better than you. You are a poor excuse for a man—for a person.

I'm so alone. The little child in me is still waiting for her Daddy to come home to be with her. To hold her and help her with all she's had to deal with in her life. She's lonely and she's afraid she might wind up like you and be alone for the rest of her life. She's so confused, it's hard to know what she wants when her basic needs for closeness and touch have never been met.

She doesn't want to be like you, Dad. You've been sick all your life and filled with anger and resentment toward everyone. You can't forgive. And now you feel that your kids are supposed to take care of you. I'm not going to take care of you. *You're* supposed to take care of *me!*

I was just a little girl, and so scared when you and Mom fought all the time. It seemed like life was going to come to an end soon. I hate you for all of that!

I don't want to do everything alone. I don't want to earn the living myself and raise the kids myself. But here I have created the same family situation for them.

I want my needs met. I want someone to be there for me. I want a man who cares about me to love me and share life with me. It seems that the one thing I want the most eludes me. It's your fault, Dad! Yes, I blame you. You were such a disappointment to me. You will die and never understand how you've affected my life and hurt me—never even care.

(Dad talking): Elizabeth, I feel about you the way I always have. I didn't know how to be a father. I was scared and inadequate, and your mother nagged me all the time. I had never been around girls much, and I had no idea what to do.

I think you're being unfair to judge me so harshly. I tried to do my best. I stuck around more than I wanted to, because of you girls. It was hell for me too, you know.

What happened happened. I couldn't help it. I had to find some escape somewhere, and the only fun around was with other women besides your mother. I never dated much in school, and we were married so young. Your mother kept saying she wanted a divorce, so we finally got one. We had no happiness together. There was no future in it for either of us.

No, I didn't give much thought to how my actions were affecting you and your sister. You were "just kids" to me then, and it was none of your business, I figured. I'm sorry I hurt you, but you hurt me too. You always pushed me away. Then you went away and left me, just like your mother. You hardly even talk to me anymore.

(Me again): Dad, I hate it when you hold me down and tickle me. I hate it so much I could kill you. I hate it when you say, "If only I were twenty years younger." What would you do, Dad, if you were twenty years younger?

I can't stand it when you refer to black people as "nigger." I hated you when you said you would come home and make it hell on earth for us. We were just kids!

I can't stand it when you yell and swear and smoke. I resent your not letting me drive the car after I got my license. I hate it that you screwed around and Mom made me drive around to find you with another woman. I hate it that I married a man who was just like you.

I hate it when you make fun of God and religion. I hate your ignorance. I hate the way you treat the dog, letting him stay chained outside in freezing weather. I hate when you hunt and kill animals, and when you made us eat squirrel and rabbit. And I hate your always saying you're going to shoot someone.

It hurts me when you yell at Mom and make her cry. It hurts me that you never play with us. I feel hurt that you ignored Alicia when she came home from the hospital. I hated it when you hit her with the belt. I was so afraid when you fought with Mom. I would put the pillow over my ears trying not to hear you, but I would still hear.

I'm afraid that I'll never heal all this stuff and my life will never be what I want. I'm afraid I'll never have a good husband. I'm afraid I'll attract someone like you again.

I'm sorry we couldn't communicate. I'm sorry we didn't have a good relationship. I regret that I just don't want to be around you now.

All I ever wanted was a Daddy who loved me. All I ever wanted was to be loved and accepted just for who I am. All I ever wanted was to be happy with my family. All I ever wanted was for my children to be happy.

All I ever wanted was to be a close family and go to church and pray together and have fun together. I deserve to have a good relationship with a man. I deserve to have a good man for a husband.

I forgive you, Dad. I know you didn't understand yourself. I guess deep down, I love you just because you are my father. Forgive me for not being able to be around you; it hurts too much to see who you are. I hope that someday you will be able to find happiness for yourself. I know I am working hard to come to peace with my past and discover my own happiness.

Feedback: It's hard to believe all that was still inside me after all these years! No wonder I've been a miserable person pretending to function "normally," but hurting so badly inside!

Closing the chapter on her painful childhood represented the healing of a long-suffering wound, the truth of which was hidden until this writing. Once her truth was out in the open, an acknowledged awareness of the ability to stand up for herself in other situations began to emerge.

The following piece was a powerful catalyst for the writer as it confirmed her own growth. It exposed a behavior which she later identified as reactionary. She had continually reacted to the partners in her life, instead of being in charge and living from her truth.

I Remember Her

I remember her. The woman who loved all those "hims." The woman who knew how to give herself away and did it quite well. The woman who hid in the corner and cried and prayed to be loved. Who on the outside looked like she knew she was good enough to be cherished, but on the inside was afraid she wasn't. The woman whose purpose was to be loved by a man so that she could dance around Him, the Maypole, the Anchor, the Reason for All Existence.

I remember her pain. I remember her desires. I was with her when she said no, then yes, then no but meant yes. When the fear of not being loved woke her screaming. When a man with a very kind touch sent her shivers full of hope and unfounded, unreasonable dreams.

I stood there and watched and hoped that she would survive as she finally said NO meaning no, and then turned in every direction looking for something to hold on to; any thing, any reason, any purpose. Drowning in an ocean with no footing in sight. When she found nothing, I cried with her as she lay still for minutes, then hours, then days, looking at nothing, seeing nothing, feeling . . . pain.

I remember her. But she has gone now, and only visits occasionally when I least expect it. I am that woman. I am that woman who is now alone, yet feels joy for no reason. Who now holds on to nothing and has no purpose but to be. I am alone now as I feel . . . love, for I have forgotten how to give myself away and I demand to be cherished because I know that I am good enough.

BE ALL OF WHO YOU ARE—CELEBRATE!

There is one question you will have to answer before you die— was I all of who I could be?

At the beginning of this book you figuratively began a journey that has passed through many stations. You have been encouraged to pay attention to where you are going, what you are seeing, and to always look for the joy along the way. Now you are pulling up to the final destination—celebration of who you are. "How can I make this celebration a constant part of my life?" you may ask. One way I have found is in writing to my-*self*, to accept total responsibility for all I create—to become the actualized dreamer.

Situations you may explore to maintain the actualized dreamer state include:

Preparation: phone calls, meetings, travel

Creation: new houses, jobs, cars, friends, mind-states

Resolution: any situation that presents itself

Knowledge: inner knowing

Wisdom: cause and effect

Truth: the truth will set you free

Joy of Celebration: Master Role—modeling

As an actualized dreamer, you are no longer letting life happen to you—you are determining or choosing your own life. You are creating a life of joy and celebration.

On the Day That I Am . . .

On the day that I am sixty I will become outrageous.

After all these years of being nice and perfect and good at everything, I won't be anymore. I will wear tennis shoes to church on Sunday and then come home and cook the spaghetti ouch dente. I may even burn the morning toast now and then.

When I go to the ball game I will sing the "Star Spangled Banner" as loud as I can, very Francis Scott off-Key. When it rains I will wear things that sparkle. Especially when it rains will I sparkle.

I will not lie about my age. After all, I have paid dearly for each and every year.

The day after my birthday I will begin my own version of the Rotation Diet: chocolate chip cookies to Snickers bars to Häagen Daz.

There will be murder mysteries at midnight and popcorn for breakfast and no more funny little gray suits in the office. The pearls can go back to Mother Oyster and I will pop out of my shell all funky and jingly and when it comes right down to it, I may put taps on my shoes and dance all the way to the mailbox.

I will say ho hum to Dan Rather, glance askew at Barbara and Brokaw. But Saturday Night Live will jive.

And so will I.

The actualized dreamer is the active participant, boldly involved in life and living the truth. For me life is to be lived and recorded. The joy, the celebration, the enthusiasm are all alive within each of us, ready to spring forward and dance. The spirit of the actualized dreamer has a playful, childlike quality that helps to create the rhythm and flow of your dance. The following experience was recorded by the writer as a moment to celebrate and cherish for all time.

Will You Marry Me?

Married? Married! I'm getting married! White lace and promises—I do, I do, oh God, I do. And now he does too. His beautiful face, smiling eyes, gentle kiss. "Will you marry me?" he says. He looks so playful—he knows how long I've waited. He is truly the cat that ate the canary at this moment. I stammer and stutter—"You're kidding, aren't you?" "Will you marry me?" he says it again. Now he's really enjoying himself—does he know how he looks to me as he says those words—what worlds of promises and hopes and dreams I see in his eyes? What a blissfully happy connection I feel with him? Does he see the dreams and promises in my eyes for him?

"Yes, yes, well sure," I say. "Great," he says. Is this how the universe was created—a "pop" and there it was out of nothing? I couldn't be any more startled. He loves me, he really loves me —what a great practice run our 12 years together has been.

As he leaves my side and goes back to his book—can you believe it—I feel like my life has changed, completely, dramatically and for the better. A warm glow begins in my center and spreads with infinite gentleness throughout my body. I feel so tender and loved, so cared for and so chosen, so perfect and special. So this is life, scared and tender, true and deep. So this is commitment, strong and caring, gentle and quiet. I think I'm going to like this.

My last question to you is—will you celebrate with me and journal for joy?

Suggested Reading List
for Enjoyment and Expansion

Adams, Kathleen. *Journey to the Self: Twenty-Two Paths to Personal Growth*. Warner Books, 1990.

Anthony, Robert. *Dr. Robert Anthony's Advanced Formula for Total Success*. Berkley, 1988.

Bach, Richard. *The Bridge Across Forever: A True Love Story*. Morrow, 1984.

_____. *Illusions: The Adventures of a Reluctant Messiah*. Delacorte, 1977.

_____. *Jonathan Livingston Seagull*. Macmillan, 1970.

Baldwin, Christina. *Life's Companion*. Berkley, 1991.

_____. *Journal Writing as a Spiritual Quest*. Bantam Books, 1990.

_____. *One to One: Self-Understanding Through Journal Writing*. M. Evans, 1977.

Blanchard, Kenneth, & Spencer Johnson. *The One Minute Manager*. Berkley, 1987.

Borysenko, Joan. *Guilt Is the Teacher, Love Is the Lesson*. Warner Books, 1990.

_____. *Minding the Body, Mending the Mind*. Addison-Wesley Pub. Co., 1987.

Bryant, Jean. *Anyone Can Write*. Whatever, 1985.

Campbell, Joseph. *The Power of Myth*. Doubleday, 1988.

Capacchione, Lucia. *The Creative Journal: The Art of Finding Yourself*. Newcastle, 1989.

_____. *Lighten Up Your Body—Lighten Up Your Life*. Newcastle, 1990.

Chapman, Joyce. *Live Your Dream: Discover and Achieve Your Life Purpose—A Step-By-Step Program*. Newcastle, 1990.

Cole-Whittaker, Terry. *How to Have More in a Have-Not World*. Rawson Associates, 1983.

_____. *The Inner Path from Where You Are to Where You Want to Be*. Rawson Associates, 1986.

_____. *What You Think of Me Is None of My Business*. Oak Tree Publications, 1982.

De Angelis, Barbara. *How to Make Love All the Time*. Macmillan, 1987.

Dychtwald, Ken. *Bodymind*. J. P. Tarcher, 1986.

Dyer, Wayne W. *Gifts from Eykis*. Pocket Books, 1984.

_____. *Pulling Your Own Strings*. Avon, 1979.

_____. *Your Erroneous Zones*. Avon, 1977.

Foundation for Inner Peace. *A Course in Miracles*. Foundation for Inner Peace, 1975.

Fox, Emmet. *The Emmet Fox Treasury*. Harper & Row, 1979.

_____. *The Mental Equivalent*. Unity School of Christianity, 1984.

Frank, Anne. *Anne Frank: The Diary of a Young Girl*. Doubleday, 1967.

Fankl, Viktor. *Man's Search for Meaning*. Washington Square Press, 1984.

Fromm, Erich. *The Art of Loving*. Harper & Row, 1974.

Gawain, Shakti, and Laurel King. *Living in the Light*. Whatever, 1986.

Goldberg, Natalie. *Writing Down the Bones: Freeing the Writer Within*. Shambhala, 1986.

Hagan, Kay Leigh. *Internal Affairs: A Journalkeeping Workbook for Self-Intimacy*. Escapadia Press, 1988.

Hammarskjöld, Dag. *Markings*. Ballantine, 1983.

Hay, Louise. *Heal Your Body*. Hay House, 1988.

Jampolsky, Gerald. *Love Is Letting Go of Fear*. Bantam, 1982.

_____. *Love Is The Answer: Creating Positive Relationships*. Bantam, 1990.

_____. *Out of the Darkness into the Light.* Bantam Books, 1989.

Jeffers, Susan. *Feel the Fear & Do It Anyway.* Harcourt Brace Jovanovich, 1987.

_____. *Opening Our Hearts to Men.* Fawcett, 1989.

Johnson, Spencer. *The One Minute Father: A Father's True Story About the Quickest Way to Teach Your Children to Like Themselves & Behave Themselves.* Morrow, 1983.

_____. *One Minute for Myself: How to Manage Your Most Valuable Asset.* Avon, 1987.

_____. *One Minute for Myself: The Secret of Caring for Yourself and Others.* Morrow, 1986.

Josefowitz, Natasha. *Is This Where I Was Going?* Warner, 1983.

_____. *Natasha's Words for Families.* Warner, 1986.

_____. *Natasha's Words for Friends.* Warner, 1986.

Jung, Carl G. *Memories, Dreams, Reflections.* Random House, 1965.

Klauser, Henriette A. *Writing on Both Sides of the Brain: Breakthrough Techniques for People Who Write.* Harper & Row, 1986.

MacLaine, Shirley. *Dancing in the Light.* Bantam, 1986.

_____. *Out on a Limb.* Bantam, 1983.

Mallon, Thomas. *A Book of One's Own: People and Their Diaries.* Ticknor & Fields, 1984.

Neiditz, Minerva. *On the Way.* Paper Moon Press, 1988.

Nin, Anaïs. *The Diary of Anaïs Nin,* Volumes I–VI. Harcourt Brace Jovanovich, 1975–1986.

Pennebaker, James W. *Opening Up: The Healing Power of Confiding in Others.* William Morrow and Company, Inc., 1990.

Price, John Randolph. *The Superbeings.* Quartus, 1981.

Progoff, Ira. *At a Journal Workshop: The Basic Text and Guide for Using the Intensive Journal.* Dialogue House Library, 1975.

Rainer, Tristine. *The New Diary: How to Use a Journal for Self-Guidance and Expanded Creativity.* Tarcher, 1978.

Ray, Sondra. *I Deserve Love.* Celestial Arts, 1987.

Reid, Clyde H. *Dreams: Discovering Your Inner Teacher.* Harper & Row, 1983.

Shaevitz, Marjorie Hansen. *The Superwoman Syndrome.* Warner, 1985.

Simons, George. *Keeping Your Personal Journal.* Ballantine, 1986.

Simonton, Carl; Simonton-Matthews, Stephanie; Creighton, James. *Getting Well Again: A Step-by-Step, Self-Help Guide to Overcoming Cancer for Patients and Their Families.* J. P. Tarcher, 1978.

Stoddard, Alexandra. *Living a Beautiful Life: Five Hundred Ways to Add Elegance, Order, Beauty & Joy to Every Day of Your Life.* Avon, 1988.

Thoreau, Henry David. *The Journal of Henry D. Thoreau.* Princeton University Press, 1984.

Viscott, David. *I Love You, Let's Work It Out.* Simon & Schuster, 1987.

_____. *The Viscott Method: A Revolutionary Program for Self-Analysis & Self-Understanding.* Houghton Mifflin, 1984.

Wakefield, Dan. *The Story of Your Life: Writing a Spiritual Autobiography.* Beacon Press, 1990.

Watts, Alan W. *The Book: On the Taboo Against Knowing Who You Are.* Random House, 1972.

_____. *Cloud Hidden, Whereabouts Unknown: A Mountain Journal.* Random House, 1965.

Joyce Chapman, M.A., is a teacher, trainer, consultant, motivational leader, and author of LIVE YOUR DREAM. She has been a dedicated journaler for more than a decade. She is devoted to living life as fully and joyfully as possible while assisting others in reaching their highest potential.

Joyce, as a teacher and teacher trainer for eighteen years, holds a California Lifetime Teaching Credential, and a master's degree in Counseling Psychology. She resides in Southern California with her husband of thirty-seven years. She is the mother of four grown children and grandmother of seven.

Through her company, Joyce makes available "Journaling for Joy" and "Live Your Dream" workshops. For information on this, and on her corporate and private consulting services, her speaking engagements, and facilitating journaling groups, write to:

www.joycechapman.com

Made in the USA
Charleston, SC
06 February 2014